PERSEVERE OVERCOME WIN

Super POWers That Will Give Your Child the EDGE in Life

By: Shaun "SF" Banks

www.kidsthatpow.com

Edited By: April Wright

Additional Consultation By: Maureen West

SF. Banks Publishing House

ISBN 978-0-692-81916-6

In life, we all experience challenges. These opportunities require us to learn how to persevere and overcome in order to win. The sooner, we start teaching these concepts to more of our future generation, the faster we'll see them thinking and dreaming bigger—capturing their most valued visions. The future is bright. Life has been designed for us to realize our dearest passions.

"It's a great time to be ALIVE!" –SF. BANKS

I AM CREED:

I am strong, I am free

I can be whatever I see

I am smart and have the heart

To finish what I start

No fear here, I have power

I'm a winner, not a coward

I have faith, so I decree

VICTORY, VICTORY!

Forward

By: Sharon Manning, Retired teacher of 27 years.

At a time when parents, schools and youth programs are searching for viable solutions to keep their children competitive and on track for a healthy and prosperous future, *Persevere Overcome Win (P.O.W.)* empowers its readers with skills to develop youth. Armed with compassion, commitment and his own self-discipline, Shaun provides readers with familiar skills that are simple to implement and rewarding for parents, teachers, or anyone who works with children.

I was always amazed at Shaun's level of self-discipline and focus. He worked hard for years developing his own self-defense skills. When he began his own self-defense school I was not surprised. When I attended his belt tests and I would watch large numbers of students demonstrate with such tenacity, to prove they had learned each level, I saw proud students and parents. Parents trusted his teaching style because it delivered results. When Camp Warrior King (CWK) was developed, I saw the same sense of commitment and discipline displayed. Hours of juggling staff development, planning and research, resulted in weeks of learning, traveling and fun…fun…fun for children of all ages and nationalities. Parents joined in attended events making CWK a large, extended family.

POW has been birthed over many years and many hours of thinking and rethinking how to best deliver the skills that are introduced to you here. (The late night phone calls and loss of sleep were worth every minute☺). I have been a parent and an educator for many years and I found myself excited reading about the strategies as I underlined many key points, and nodded my head in agreement.

Parents, teachers and all people who interact with children, you are given a new responsibility. You've been deemed vital to the development of this generation of children. They will be the leaders that we need for our world tomorrow, and POW shows you how to develop students for success.

TABLE OF CONTENTS

Be sure to maximize the advantages of buying this book!

*Take your students, staff and school to the next level. Schedule a presentation for your next professional development workshop.

*Get FREE training videos and access more resources on our website.

*Let us know which concepts helped you, your team and/or your children most. We want to hear from you.

*Do you have a friend, co-worker or know of a school/program the information in this book can provide value to? Share the love and please let them know about this book and the valuable information.

Visit Kidsthatpow.com

Call (678)-408-2053

PO BOX 87401, COLLEGE PARK, GA 30337

1

FIRST THINGS FIRST:

Housekeeping & Maximizing Results from POW

> *"I have never encountered any children in any group who are not geniuses. There is no mystery on how to teach them. The first thing you do is treat them like human beings and the second thing you do is love them."* --Dr. Asa Hilliard.

Some of you may be taken aback with the first sentence of Dr. Hilliard's quote. You may have actually said to yourself "Humph, he must not have met some of the kids I've encountered." LOL! While your opinion may have some validity, allow me to share something with you:

Perception is the key. What you think will be, will be. Do you remember your favorite teacher, coach, or friend? Quickly think of your best memory with them that will make you smile or laugh. Aren't you thankful there was someone willing to create a lasting and positive mark in your life in spite of your imperfections? Isn't it awesome this person perceived the best in you regardless of what you thought about yourself or regardless of what you actually were?

People, like the one who impacted your life, I call VTLs (pronounced Vitals); it stands for Village Team Leaders. VTLs are adults qualified either through experience and or education to positively develop children towards success (parents, teachers, counselors, administrators and all other professionals and people who interact with children). By picking up this book you're a VTL. You were meant to read this book. You're someone who wants to impact the lives of children in a greater way—correct? How do I know? Well, the title of this book is very direct in regards to its focus. So, thank you for choosing this book. Now, let's get to work and direct some kids toward self-realization, shall we?

If you like what you read, or most of what you read, I'd love to hear from you and get to know you better and find out what you've learned—even better, post a picture or video on my Facebook wall at **www.facebook.com/sfbanks.**

A few housekeeping points!

Note: for the duration of this book, unless noted, adults who work with children or raise them will be referred to as VTL's. When I refer to your children, I mean the children you're servicing or raising. Got it? Great!

Allow me to share a few thoughts about what to expect from this book, who should be reading it, and what I expect from you. It's important to know what you're getting into up front.

First, my objective is not to tell you how to raise your children—you know them much better than I do. I am imparting information that will change your life and the lives you touch forever, if you put the information to proper use. The Ideas, recommendations and solutions in this book, I have developed, used and taught for over 20 years to help improve the lives of thousands of families whom I've personally worked with, who've attend my Spring, Summer or Fall development camps, attended my workshops, watched my videos online and/or have received personal consultation. I have spent personal time and studied under some of the best motivators, personal developers and business people in the world.

I have personally consulted all family make-ups including foster parents, those who adopted children, custodial guardians (aunts, uncles, siblings and grandparents) and same sex marriage households. The most important aspect, regardless of your household make-up, is the unconditional love and quality time you give your children.

In this time frame I have also consulted teachers, administrators, counselors, professors and mentors on strategies to improve and/or implement positive performance in children. The same strategies that work on children, are also effective for those in business, sales, in school or any profession where one is looking to reach peak performance and have an edge over the competition.

Second, having “bad” children is not a requirement to read POW, nor are you a bad parent if you’re reading it. The best are always looking for ways to improve and modify where needed. Michael Jordan practiced and studied film relentlessly even at the height of his game—the reason he maintained an edge over the competition. Likewise, great parents are always looking for ways to become better for their children. If you picked up this book, you represent a group of the best. “Bad” parents won’t read this book—most of them believe they already know it all and find out otherwise when time has all but run out. If you’re seeking ways to maximize your child’s potential and give them a greater competitive edge in life—you should read this book.

POW is designed for adults looking to enhance their children’s performance in any area if they’re top performers or aspiring ones—doesn't matter. This book is based on timeless, proven principles which have been broken down so you can teach them more easily. It is packed with rich content and ideas to show you the most powerful ways to develop your children's minds so they're thinking like winners consistently.

Photo: Speaking to a group of young men about the importance of a dream and having a plan. They were a sharp group of talented guys.

If you are experiencing challenges with your children, POW will give you more than hope. This book will give you ideas, recommendations and solutions to redirect your child in the direction you want them to go. Are you working with children who: lack confidence, need better work ethic, lack perseverance, lack focus or a dream? Are you working with children who need a more productive attitude, suffer from peer pressure, lack of interest in activities and/or need to learn about money and ways to make it and keep it? This book is excellent for you.

Third, Persevere Overcome Win is interactive. There will be lots of chances for you to get more content, see training videos, participate in live online events and register for upcoming workshops, youth conferences, our personal development summer camp and personal consultation service.

Fourth, this book is NOT designed to diagnose or treat children with severe behavior issues or learning disabilities. I am not a psychologist or psychiatrist however my strategies will assist your children to face difficult challenges, fight through them and win just as it has helped thousands of other children, adults and working professionals.

Fifth, POW will give you more responsibilities to add to your already hectic list. If you're a parent or work directly with children—I'm sure you can handle it. You must be an active reader, meaning do the exercises in the book and do the suggested work outside the book. It will be so worth it when you see your children becoming and doing what you knew was possible for them. We get out what we put into something, children are no different.

As in the movie Pain & Gain with Mark Wahlberg, Johnny Wu says: "Do be a doer…don't be a don'ter!" It's a hilarious scene but the concept is very applicable. So, do read the book, work the system and tell your friends and colleagues when you find useful information.

This system works if you work it. Put forth effort if you really wish to see change in your kids. Don't throw this book down after reading a few pages because you feel you don't have time to do the work. Let me tell you, in this era of distractions and misguided information, this is one of the best places to invest your time. Don't miss out on valuable information that may save the lives of children you come in contact with.

It may mean less binge watching of your favorite crime or reality show, attending fewer Monday Night Football bar parties and sometimes missing your highly anticipated golf, tennis or soccer match. It may mean replacing some not so good habits with better ones, replacing some not so good influences with positive ones. Remember, you're seeking change and change sometimes causes temporary discomfort in exchange for long-term satisfaction. Change starts with you.

Persevere, Overcome and Win: the Super POWers you must teach your children to give them the EDGE in life, show you highly effective ways to remove roadblocks and positively change the lives of your children! It's a life-changing, sure-fire how-to book guiding you through what I call super powers that can transform and catapult your children into a capacity where they're capable, confident and successful members of society.

In this book, I assist you in creating effective solutions and strategies to the many challenges you'll face molding children in today's world. This book will excite you, motivate you and get you hungry enough to do something about the obstacles you want to see children overcome. POW will get your creativity flowing with ideas to help you serve the children better.

POW serves as a vessel to give you concepts to ponder that will hopefully open up a dialogue between you and God...there, you will find the greatest solutions to develop the children in your care.

Persevere Overcome Win!

If you want your children to have the edge in life, they must do what other children don't do. YOU must do what other adults are not willing to do. Photo: a group of our students completing assignments in their summer workbooks.

HOW TO MAXIMIZE YOUR RESULTS FROM POW

Understand this: Every child is a superhero already. Many of them at birth go through things you and I couldn't handle, yet come out without bruise or burn. Some children are abused in various ways and/or neglected by the ones they love and cherish most, yet still find a way to show up with a smile on their faces and laughter in their hearts. Unfortunately, others become infected by their situations and express it through violence, anger and ignorance.

Like a superhero, each kid is one of a kind and carries his/her own set of abilities and weaknesses. For example, Superman with all his superhuman strength and abilities, constantly gets defeated by the small things (kryptonite) and cannot figure out how to overcome or get rid of them. Batman is a recluse who lacks healthy relationships. Spiderman is a hopeless romantic; the Incredible Hulk suffers from severe anger issues.

Super POW©--the round little guy on the front cover, is our mascot. Super POW© promotes the inner power of kids, their families and their villages to fight through all situations, regardless of the circumstances and arise victorious.

As a VTL, we must value children's unique abilities as they are and NOT as we'd like them to be.

How to read this book:

1. You can open Persevere Overcome Win and read only about the specific issues you think your child should improve on--no problem. What about the qualities you haven't thought about? How many kids have we seen with great potential and opportunities, struggle due to one or two roadblocks that if removed would catapult

them to a higher level? My research has shown me the children who perform best in school, at home and in life have learned to sharpen all their skills, not just one or two.

For example, it will be useless to teach children to have great money management skills if they lack work ethic, because they'll never work hard enough to have any money to manage. A key is to develop the whole child. POW provides strategies to do it.

Read this book with a pen, highlighter, notebook or your phone notes section handy. When you read this book, ideas are going to flow into your mind, you must write them down to review them later. You may occasionally have an "AMEN," moment and that's when you should highlight the passage and dog-ear the page so you can read it again and share it with a friend.

2. Expect to get an idea. The words I've written are not as powerful as the ideas that will be created in your mind when you read them. Each time you read my book, you should be able to formulate unique ideas for the children you're serving.

3. After you've read the book a few times, use Super POW as a reference tool to assist you in tailor-making the most effective, practical and long-lasting solutions available.

Super POW gives you an arsenal of ideas like never before. If you're a first time teacher or been teaching for 30 years, this book will enhance your performance in the classroom and at home because the strategies here help you teach to the whole child. If you're a parent, counselor or someone who loves to work with kids, this book is right for you. No more reading never to find a real, workable solution. There are real solutions in this book that can be used with a child in any socio-economic background or upbringing.

More so, an overwhelming amount of children are not learning these skills at home or at school—it shows. There is a child who needs you to read this book, so you can use the solutions to save his/her life. After reading this book you will have tools to help you change lives and get lost children back on track. Life is filled with situations and circumstances which require us to **P**ersevere **O**vercome and **Win**. Some situations are very small requiring little effort and others are gigantic requiring every ounce of faith, will power and strength. Regardless, history has proven over and over that we can make it through any situation and defeat any giant, PERIOD. You, too, are more than a conqueror. There's nothing that can stop you and your child if you want it badly enough. Implement with a vengeance and ONLY BELIEVE. The time is now to develop children who POW!

KEYS TO OPEN THE DOORS

The Five keys to develop kids who POW!

When you change and grow, your child will do the same. How fast you develop will determine at what rate your child will develop, too.

Some of the best solutions are the ones you'll create with your child. You and your child are on the same team with the same goal in mind: TO WIN! In order to do so, you will need to learn the four keys to developing children who POW.

I find it very interesting when I hear parents or people working with kids say, "I'm not your friend, I'm your parent," or an educator might say, "I'm not your friend, I'm your teacher!" Well, if you're not their friend then who is? Now, I understand the context of the phrase, but let me assure you the kid you're talking to does not. Who can be a better friend to a child than the person or persons who should know them best?

Webster's Dictionary defines a friend as a supporter or well-wisher. Are you not supporting your children and wishing them well? The VTL, especially a parent or guardian should be a child's best friend.

All friendships have boundaries, right? If your best friend borrows money from you and never pays you back, aren't there going to be some "consequences and repercussions," as the late Bernie Mack used to say? Of course! Chances are this person will be the last one invited to your next BBQ right? LOL! Point is it's completely OK to be your child's friend and still enforce standards, set parameters and establish discipline in the home or school. Remember, you're the best friend; no one has a greater investment and stands more to lose than you.

My parents have always been my best friends—and still are. However, it never stopped my mom from going Madea on me when I acted up and it certainly didn't deter my dad. Jay-Z the rapper says it best: "Friend or Foe?" If you're going to be your child's friend, shouldn't you be the best one they'll ever have? If not, then you're the other guy right? Good luck with that.

The Utility Belt

It's time to put on your utility belt! Imagine Batman trying to carry all those gadgets in his arms while jumping from building to building fighting bad guys! Those little Batman ninja stars would be lost everywhere, and, worse, they'd get their butts kicked. Why does Batman use a utility belt? One word…Convenience. It simply makes his job easier. The four keys make up your utility belt. The five principles I'm going to teach are the tools to carry on your belt. As you study the super powers in this volume, you'll notice that each one is easier to use if it's implemented in conjunction with the five keys. The keys are:

ONE: Have a winning **ATTITUDE**

TWO: Teach by Doing. Be the **EXAMPLE**

THREE: Teach with **PATIENCE**

FOUR: Teach through **LOVE**

FIVE: Have a **PLAN**

NOW STOP…Reflect a moment and highlight what you just read. Read them again and again until you memorize them. The five keys are just that important.

Persevere Overcome Win!

The five keys to developing children who POW are more than a notion. These tools require us to think before we act (something we can all do a better job of, LOL). As long as you interact with kids, you should practice using the five keys. Additionally, you can use the same keys when interacting with a spouse, co-worker or relative! But for now, let's stick with the kiddies; I don't want you throwing my book down just yet, LOL!

ATTENTION! YOU ARE ABOUT TO READ A "NON-STARTER!"

Here it is:

If you cannot make a concerted effort to follow the five keys to developing children who POW, then our new relationship is over! We're not even going to start this affair, because we'll be wasting our time.

POW teaches adults how to develop into better leaders while simultaneously showing us how to teach children to use the awesome powers that lie inside them. If you're not willing or ready to develop yourself, if your feel you already have all the answers, what makes you think you can get a child to develop?

When you change and grow, your child will do the same. How fast you develop will determine at what rate your child will develop. So, we have a deal that you agree to keep striving to change and get better? AWESOME! Please continue. ☺

The better you become at using the four keys the faster you'll see results. You'll also become a more likeable person (for what it's worth to you).

Key #1: Have a Winning Attitude!

One of the biggest keys to success in any area is having a winning attitude. Without a winning attitude you will not succeed in anything… no matter what it is, business, school, home, romance. Your attitude is an expression of the inner you, and people are attracted to a positive attitude and driven away by a negative one. A winning attitude is a choice and a matter of perspective.

People can decide if they're winners or losers regardless of the outcomes they face. There's a big difference between losing and actually being a loser. One describes an instance and the other describes what is consistent.

Having a winning attitude is a habit and it takes effort to develop. If your attitude is lousy, it will infect the children around you and cause their attitude to become lousy as well.

An effective VTL must develop a winning attitude in order to invoke positive self-realization in children. Many children will struggle with realizing who they can be, who they actually are, and who they are not. The right attitude can help you push life's challenges where the wrong attitude may not. An example of a winning attitude is what many children need to see.

Shelly L. is a single mother of four children who worked at a department store outside of Baltimore. Her husband died in a tragic car accident when their youngest son, Jackson was two. Most of her family lived back in Chicago, so Shelly was left in a challenging position to raise four children alone. After burying her husband, Shelly felt it was almost impossible to bear the load of raising her children alone and often contemplated separating the kids, sending them to live with distant relatives. In spite of her fears, Shelly decided to keep her children together, work during the day and pursue finishing her education at night. Although a challenging path, Shelly weathered the storm and eventually got her bachelors and masters degrees and works on a high administrative level at a community college. Two of her children are in college, one is in the Navy and Jackson is in trade school. What helped her? Shelly says she made a **commitment** to never give up on her children; that if the kids could see her overcome hardships and still raise a family—they would be able to believe nothing is impossible. Although it was hard at times, Shelly believed that challenging things happen to people everyday, but it's how you handle those challenges--no matter how severe that determines the outcome of our lives.

Key #2: Teach by Doing. Be the Example!

Being in personal development and performance enhancement over the years, I've encountered thousands of families. I cannot stress how important it is for adults to be the example of what they wish to see from their children. I've learned that 9 times out of 10 if I want to understand why children have a certain behavior—just meet the people who are influencing their lives! Oh, boy! You can truly judge a tree by the fruit it bears.

With the support of an incredible staff, I run a personal development summer camp named Camp Warrior King (CWK; campwarriorking.com). Every summer hundreds of fired-up kids from all social-economic backgrounds get together for about 9-10 weeks for the most fun they have all year! We horseback ride, take long trips, do archery, shoot rifles and do just about anything we find fun and safe for the kids.

We take "Be the Example" to heart when it comes to our activities. One of the best ways to help children have fun is to have fun yourself...and we do! Photo: The craziest game of Paintball ever!

At CWK, we have a ton of really talented children and every once in a while we have campers who want to take their talents too far. "One time at summer camp" (#americanpie LOL), we had to stop a little girl from "dropping it like it's hot," during a dance off and just about every other time we played music. The young lady's mom couldn't understand our concern. The parent started by saying, "What's the problem with my child dancing? She can't dance?" I'm like: "Well ma'am, there's nothing wrong with dancing, however I have concerns with *the way* she's dancing at camp.

At this point, I could see the mom's horns begin to protrude from under her bonnet :-\ . The mom takes a deep breath, exhales like she's obviously annoyed, turns to her little girl and says, "What we do at home, stays at home. I don't care what you see me do. Do as I say and not as I do!" The look on my face was like: 😐 "Wow, did she just say that?!"

Parents, I hate to disappoint you, but the "what we do at home, stays at home," line doesn't work. Your children will say and do what they see and hear you say and do at home. Surprise!

Also, "Do as I say, not as I do," the typical adult response when trying to justify an action or remark that's normally considered inappropriate—also a joke. Good luck with using both of those. Kids are great copycats and are able to repeat your actions at the most embarrassing times! You may want to remove these examples from your arsenal!

Make an effort to let your children see you do only things you want them to do. When I teach an SF Performance Enhancement workshop, I teach that leaders lead by example. It's my philosophy that if you want people to do something, you must first do it, and they will follow.

Credibility is an essential key to building trust. Dads, if you promise to spend the weekend with your kid(s) by going fishing—do it. Principals, if you've promised the basketball team new uniforms—get it done. Remember, kids have the memory of an elephant (at least, when they want something). They don't forget just because you've stopped mentioning it.

Stop right now and think of something an adult promised you as a kid that he/she failed to deliver on. How did that make you feel? Isn't it funny we can still remember those things? Get the point?

The results are astounding when VTLs teach by doing because it's so rare to see anyone doing it nowadays. Most people just teach by talking and talking and talking. So, let's talk less and **do more.**

KEY #3 Teach With Patience:

This third point is sometimes easy to lose (pun intended). Don't think so? Try teaching a small child how to tie his/her shoes, ride a bike or eat using utensils, and you'll soon find out! At some point along the way you may have even thought, "This kid is in for a hard life, if he can't put his shoes on the right feet…OMG, it's been five minutes already and she still can't figure out how to make bunny ears with her shoe laces, arrgh!" Relax, breathe in…breath out.

Patience with children is more than not getting upset; it's the idea that you're going to be consistent and persistent in doing your part knowing that one day the child will catch on. Patience is never losing hope that a child can pivot into a better behavior pattern. I've personally witnessed kids who could not control their anger; then after a series of strategic development exercises and implementing my system were able to manage themselves in a better fashion.

We should not expect a child who has years of social behavioral issues to change in a few days. Many adults get frustrated when a child doesn't magically change after a teacher conference—yeah, right. For some children, their negative behavior is a way to manipulate and or protect themselves. For other children, there are layers of hurt and disappointments that may have to be rolled back first. It will take time and the support of a patient, determined VTL for results to manifest. But rest assured, improvement will come with **determination** from a VTL and the cooperation from the child.

There are some VTLs who seriously lack patience. Their tempers are quick and their ability to understand how children think is low. These people should not work with children. It's not that these folks are bad people, they're just not the right fit to work with a child. If you don't know what I'm talking about, take a look at your evening news. It's full of scenarios where adults have "lost it" when dealing with a child.

KEY #4: Teach Through Love:

It's been said, "People don't care how much you know, they want to know how much you care." Regardless of what we're teaching, the children we lead must feel that the source of our instruction is from a place of unconditional love…love is how you gain trust, and through trust you accomplish change. Children won't do anything you need them to do if they don't have a level of trust and know your intentions are genuine.

Many of you reading this book may be seeking knowledge to help children who aren't your own. Let me tell you, love is still the principle thing. Its love that will carry you when your knowledge fades, your patience runs thin and your mind says "Give up." Love is the greatest principle. Love never fails. (**1 Corinthians 13:8)**

It is not hard to walk in love when you know who you are and whose you are. Love is the superior strength. The world perceives love as weakness—WRONG! Believers know God is love.

Some people have a hard time showing love not because they are mean people, rather they have a hard time trusting. Now, don't get me wrong, some kids are harder to love than others. When children know you truly love them, they know you won't hurt them. At this point they will begin to entertain your ideas about change.

Love means that your desire to see a child succeed is greater than what the statistics, co-workers, social workers or even their parents may say. It's greater than your fears. As long as a child is willing to entertain change by showing effort and marked progress, we have a shot. If a child is unwilling to change—we should still love him/her, but move our attention toward seeking a higher level of help. DON'T PANIC, your collective of VTLs is HUGE...we'll discuss that later.

Key #5 Have a Plan

Without an effective, well thought-out plan, you are a ship without a captain at the helm. Photo: On our way to our annual Cumberland Island Safari Tour.

Old adages tend to ring true: “If you fail to plan, you plan to fail.” and the cliché 5Ps, “Proper planning prevents poor performance.” If you’ve never heard these before, write these quotes down and commit them to memory. These timeless principles are applicable to just about every area of life and business. Most things you do are better with a plan and worse without one. Doctors plan procedures, sports teams discuss strategies before games, some businesses spend tens of thousands of dollars developing a plan, and so on. Plans work!

Planning or having a well thought-out strategy is essential to seeing change or developing a child. It doesn't matter how good of an attitude you have, how well you're being an example, showing patience or love, without a plan you'll work harder, experience more frustration, waste more money and eventually give up or succumb to whatever you're attempting to avoid. Without an effective, well thought-out plan you are a ship without a captain at the helm, a train in the sand or an octopus on roller-skates: a whole lot of movement with little to no progress.

I think about a kid named Steven. Steven was a talented, handsome kid from Milwaukee who loved football and was a star on his little league team before he stated getting in trouble and hanging with a bad group. As a kid, he carried a football to school and slept with one at night. Unfortunately for Steven, his father was a career criminal and his mom was addicted to on heroin. Steven lived with his grandfather most of his life. His Granddad worked on the railroad so he wasn't home, but kept food in the fridge and clothes on Steven's back. Without a plan and support, Steven ended up in and out of youth detention camps.

The last time Steven was at the detention center, he promised himself he would never come back. He had already spent too many of his young years behind bars.

While exiting the camp, a correction officer told him: "we'll keep your spot ready for when you come back."

Frustrated and mildly determined, Steven a free young man, went back to his granddad's house—but still without a plan and no support. In less than 24 months from being released, Steven the talented, handsome kid who dreamed of being a football star for the Dallas Cowboys was headed not to a detention camp this time but to prison for 10 years. His charge: Armed robbery. It has been said that when you don't have a plan, one will be created for you.

On the other hand, a great plan is like playing on a team with a winning record when you play against a team with a losing record: The odds are in your favor.

When working with children, a good plan gives you something to work with, to modify, gives you and the children you're working with hope and excitement, builds camaraderie and finally a good plan will let you know if the children are following through on their end of the bargain.

Of course a plan doesn't guarantee success, but it sure beats the odds of not having one. With or without a plan you may progress or regress, but a plan will allow you to see it faster and waste less time.

I.R.S.

IDEAS RECOMMENDATION SOLUTIONS

HOW TO HAVE A WINNING ATTITUDE:

1. **Always see the glass half full and not half empty.** Remember what I said in the beginning of the book: Perception is the key. How we view a situation is normally how it will turn out. The mind is powerful. When dealing with children, view them as having potential…not as being bad. Children know when you have a negative perception about them because it shows in your interaction with them. It's easy to detect fake people, believe it or not.

   You must **SEE IT, SPEAK IT, SEE IT**. These are the most basic steps of bringing your goals to fruition.

   A. **SEE IT:** You must first visualize in your mind's eye what it is you want to happen. Meditate on the vision until it becomes crystal clear to you. Do not proceed to the next step without a clear vision. It is written: "And the spirit of God moved upon the face of the waters." (Genesis 1:2) The Amplified

Bible says He was hovering, pondering. To ponder is to consider deeply. If God, ponders shouldn't we? Ever heard the phrase: "Think before you speak"? Once you have the vision write it down. (Habakkuk 2:2-4)

B. **SPEAK IT:** Speak aloud the vision you wrote down with faith and conviction. There is power in speaking things aloud. Speaking what you want will bring your vision from the spiritual realm into the physical realm. **You will have what you say. Good or Bad.** When God made the Heavens and the Earth, He spoke: "And God said, Let there be light…" (Genesis 1:3)

C. **SEE IT:** Put in the required effort and you will have (see) what you envisioned. "And God saw the light, that it *was* good…" (Genesis 1:4)

People with a winning attitude are confident they will have what they say. Do not ever say what you don't want. Words are powerful seeds. As a VTL you must get time alone to get a clear vision for your role in the life of the child and to "hear" where and how you should lead the child. This will strengthen your attitude and give you greater hope.

2. **Focus on the big picture.** Having the right attitude takes seeing the end at the beginning. One bad day does not equal a bad life—it's just a bad day; we all have them. Look at where you're going not so much at what you're going through.

3. **Protect your positivity.** Avoid negative-thinking people and refuse to allow negative attitudes, talking or defeatist behavior in your presence. Words are seeds of killer weeds formed from thoughts and meditations. When negative words and actions are emitted they're looking for soil to take root and grow. Do not be the soil.

4. **Practice showing a positive attitude in all situations.** Like anything good or bad, it becomes concrete through habit. When things happen, take a few seconds to analyze the situation and CHOOSE to find the positive in it or at least find peace. This is not always easy and takes practice, patience and time.

HOW TO TEACH BY DOING:

1. **Think before you act.** When you're in the presence of kids, before you do or say something ask yourself, is my current behavior something I want modeled? If not, change it.

2. **Create a team atmosphere.** Create a team atmosphere with your children or students as a way to set the standard of behavior you wish to see. For example you may say: We are the Johnsons, we don't talk with our mouths full at the dinner table." Or you may say: "We are the Crimson Tide, we don't lose to Auburn," (I like that one, ROLL, TIDE!). People, especially kids, want to feel like they're a part of a family or team (one of the reasons so many youth join gangs or use drugs). You'll notice, children will respond better because they'll have a sense of pride about what they're a part of and what it means.

3. **Reciprocity of Accountability**: If you hold kids to a standard, they will also hold you accountable to the same standard. When the tables are turned and it's your turn to be accountable, it's very important to be humble enough to say "You're right," and apologize.

This will prevent the assumption of a double standard being created.

At a local basketball game the coach for the Silver Knights gets irate because of a bad call by the referee and begins cussing and giving the middle finger. One of the players notices and mentions it after the game: "Coach owes us 50 push-ups for cursing during the game. Hey coach, we're the Knights and the Knights don't curse during the games right?"

Now, coach can say, "I'm the coach and I'm in charge," then refuse to show remorse—which will reduce his credibility with the players. Or, coach can say: "You're right team," and do the push-ups. Which one will continue to build the respect of coach's players?

HOW TO TEACH WITH PATIENCE:

1. **Be in the right frame of mind first!** Before you do anything involving teaching a child, be sure you're in the proper headspace to do it. This may seem funny, but it's important. Are you rested? Have you

prepared? Are you even in the mood? Remember, it's always better to defer to a later date than to make a mistake you may or may not be able to rebound from.

It's kind of like the first year teachers who come to their first day. They look so cute, with their brand new coffee mug, blouse or suit and their fancy pencil pouch.

By the end of the day, their nostrils are flared like a raging bull; there's runs in her stockings, he's stained another tie with mystery meat sauce and some jerk kid who just failed the reading test is rapping Gucci Mane and Future in the back of class—the uncensored versions! DON'T LOSE YOUR COOL! If you're hip, you may want to learn some Gucci or whoever's hot and rap along, or you can at least bob your head, they'll laugh, you'll laugh…it will be OK.

2. **Take a break.** Developing kids is an awesome yet sometimes very challenging task. There's nothing wrong with taking a few minutes to get some fresh air, switch lessons or have a few minutes of silence.
   Try using the old fire safety analogy of STOP, DROP AND ROLL. If things get too hot, STOP what you're

doing, DROP the issue or lesson right then and there and ROLL out! (i.e., walk away for a minute). That's so much better than yelling at the kids or degrading them. This consistent practice will also help you keep your job or from saying something you may regret later on.

3. **Get upset with the issue.** If and when you get upset, be upset with the issue and not the child. Note that children are not good or bad, they're displaying the development of good behavior or bad behavior.

   Try this response next time you find yourself upset with your child: (using his/her name) I'm not upset with you, I want to see your grades improve. How can we resolve this together? Not: "why can't you get good grades, what's wrong with you, why are you acting so stupid?" Now, I know you would never talk to a child like this, but you'd be surprised at how many people do.

TEACHING THROUGH LOVE

Love is the ultimate power. The family is where children first learn about love and how to love. A strong family bond helps fortify children's foundation. Children who are well loved, will love others.

1. **Keep the shoe on the other foot!** Always put yourself in a child's shoes. Do 3-year-olds REALLY know why they pooped on themselves right after you took them to the bathroom? No.

2. **Show love as a strength, not a weakness.** You can tell someone "No," and still love them. You correct wrong behavior out of love. You discipline children because you love them. Loving a child does not mean saying yes all the time.

3. **Don't be afraid to tell people you love them.** You'd be surprised the number of kids or adults who go days without hearing "These three words," as the great Stevie Wonder would say. They're sweet and simple. He's right.

   A lot of my staff, especially the guys, have this funny look when I tell them "Hey, I love ya!" It's this look like: "Ok, who's this weirdo, and why does he love me? He doesn't know me." After enough times of "professing my love," they'll begin to say it back. Now, that doesn't mean I won't get on their case for a poor performance, it just means I'll do it in love. ;-)

DEVELOPING A PLAN

A good plan of action or strategy will give you and the child you're helping confidence that what you're working to achieve is actually possible. When I consult families one of the first things we put together is a plan of action. My pop, who I will talk about later in this volume, taught me a great way of developing workable strategies during my freshman year at the University of Alabama (ROLL, TIDE!). I've used it to train people all over the country. Below is a thumbnail sketch of a plan. A good plan of action has several key components:

1. **Strategize.** The first part of making a plan is deciding what you want to do. An example may be: Justin is going to lose 5lbs over the next couple weeks to gain speed for his competition. Simple enough, right?

2. **Organize.** In the organization stage, you discuss what exactly you're going to do, how exactly you're going to do it and by what date and time it will be done. More detail may be needed depending on the situation. So, in this example: Justin is going to run two miles three days a week around Perkerson Park and do light strength training two days a week for the next three weeks at Big Muscles Gym; reduce his carbohydrate intake; and get to bed by 9:30pm each night.

3. **Motivate.** This section is the building of the moral stage where you may discuss the results of the plan. This is where you visualize the ending at the beginning. For example: Justin will drop the 5lbs to meet his goal weight, his speed will increase by .5

seconds and he will win the competition, and carry the state championship trophy.

4. **Implementation and Modification.** Simply put: do the plan. Procrastination and fear are plan-killers and dream-stealers. All the writing down of goals is a waste of time if you never do it. Get started immediately doing some aspect of your plan. There is always some productive thing that can be done. This is also where you make mid-course adjustments, if needed, to meet the goal.

Make sure that the plan is typed or written and that both you and the child have a copy and post it in a place that's highly visible.

3

A GOOD ATTITUDE WILL TAKE YOU WHERE A DOLLAR WON'T:

How to develop a winning attitude in your children

"A good attitude can take you where a dollar won't!" Some of our kids won this trip for displaying a winning attitude while handling certain responsibilities. I don't think many parents envisioned this when we announced a tree climbing trip.

"[Luke:] I can't believe it. [Yoda:] That is why you fail."

Earlier, we discussed the importance of Village Team Leaders having a winning attitude in life. The necessity of a winning attitude is no less important when dealing with children. Fortunately for the VTL's, it's a little easier to develop a winning attitude in children than in other adults. By and large, children haven't experienced the same amounts or severity of failures yet. Most children, whether they've been through tough times or not, are pretty optimistic. Adults tend to be more cynical.

My mother has always told me, "A good attitude will take you where a dollar won't." I've learned through experience that people are more likely to lend a helping hand to someone with a great attitude and less likely to support someone who has a nasty attitude.

In order for us to develop children's confidence, they must also have their attitude set to winning. What do I mean? Well, have you ever baked a cake? If you look at a recipe, there will normally be instructions to set the oven temperature to a desired heat. Now, when you set the temperature does the oven become hot instantly? No, you set the temperature, and then it normally takes a few minutes to arrive at the degree of heat you desire. While you wait, you continue with other instructions like mixing or prepping.

Developing the right attitude is no different. Keep in mind the children you're helping, especially if they're not your own, already have an attitude set. Your job is to develop that attitude to a higher level, and it takes time. As the children are improving in the areas of confidence, their "I can, I will," attitude will get better and better.

How to set a winning attitude in children

Most children have been programmed to follow instructions. They learn to follow instructions at home, places of worship, school, in extra-curricular activities and so on. Since that's the case, a VTL should instruct children in similar fashion in regards to helping them develop a winning attitude.

1. **Set the expectation. VTLs should set the expectation of the attitude they wish to see.**

   Children know what's expected of them everywhere else in regards to performance. Unfortunately, many of them, regardless of their socio-economic background, do not know what kind of attitude they're expected to have on a daily basis. Are they supposed to fight when they're angry, pout when they don't get their way, or celebrate at the misfortune of another?

   There is an obvious difference in children developed with a winning attitude and when they're not. Setting the expectation is letting children know what will and what will not be tolerated in regards to their attitude. The expectations you set are up to you, but regardless, they must be adhered to by the children.

When developing a winning attitude, these aspects should be included:

a. **There is no such thing as "I can't." In a winner's attitude.** Children developing their confidence must understand they can do all things—especially if they're believers. My experience has shown me that most children use the phrase "I can't" as an excuse to continue lack-luster performance. Alternatively, when children say "I can't" they're saying "I can't believe enough to see myself doing this." These internal philosophies must not be admitted into the atmosphere of a winner. DO NOT ALLOW it. When children say "I can't," you say, "Yes, you can."

b. **Kids should understand: Failing does not make them failures.** Many times, children equate failing or losing as being a failure. That can't be further from the truth. Many children are very weak when coping with failure because they've learned, mostly from fantasy, that winners always win. We know that failure teaches you lessons on how to win better and more often.

   Winners are not born, they're developed through adversity. No one has won every game, or aced every test. Sure, we don't want them to become complacent with losing, but children must learn the lessons in their own defeat in order to improve. When children learn from a loss, they have put themselves into a position to win again and again

c. **Find something positive in all situations:** In today's world, we are faced with so much negativity. Children are bombarded with adult situations way earlier than most of us were. Whether you're a VTL who decides to protect your child from adult situations or show less discretion towards exposing adult matters, finding the positive in all situations allows children to keep a fresh perspective on the life they're living.

   Keeping a positive perspective fuels a winning attitude and more often keeps children from spiraling into depression which is a harder enemy to fight. So, if you go out to eat and dinner was lousy, find the positive: Was the atmosphere nice? Was the waiter pleasant? Find something.

A winning attitude rests in an atmosphere you and the child must create together. If you and the child can share a positive outlook on the direction you're heading, doors will open up much faster.

Remember the five keys to developing kids who POW:

One - Have a winning ATTITUDE. It starts with you.

Two - Teach by Doing. Be the EXAMPLE! If your attitude is lousy, your kid's attitude may be lousy, too.

Three – Teach with PATIENCE. Allow children time to grow and develop their attitude. Remember (especially if they're not your biological children) you may have to pull back layers of negative attitudes, and you may be combating a home situation that is toxic. In this case, patience is key to an uphill climb. You may not see the results today, but rest assured your effort will not be in vain.

Four – Teach through LOVE. Love the children through their attitude transition. Don't get offended by ignorance. When you get upset, be upset with the behavior NOT the child. Your love can outlast their immaturity.

Five – Have a PLAN. Have a strategy to improve their attitude. Use the outline I presented in the earlier section to help you develop ideas.

4

INSIDE OF EACH CHILD IS A DREAM WAITING TO EXPLODE:

Getting Your Children Dreaming Bigger and More Motivated!

A space-age achiever is also a space-age dreamer. Dream small, accomplish small...dream big, accomplish bigger than you've ever imagined. Multi-Millionaire businessman and trailblazer George Halsey accomplished big. Not only that, but he knew how to get others excited about their future and to dream bigger than their status quo.

We must get kids dreaming bigger in America...no matter what it takes. To risk losing a nation of big dreamers is to risk losing our nation. The future belongs to the children. I mean...Whitney Houston told us that. Our children must be great out of the box thinkers in order to compete in a world filled with stifling competitiveness.

There is a great power in children having the liberty to be creative and believe they have no limits. How else will we find the cures for diseases like cancer and AIDS if people are not dreaming past what others say is, or is not, possible? Children do not have limits except for the ones they are conditioned to have by the people surrounding them.

What is a dream? A worthy dream can be an idea, yearning, or desire that comes with a vision detailing its fruition topped with a deep desire to implement it. A dream that doesn't come with a deep desire to implement the vision is merely a thought.

Why are dreams important to developing children? For one, children have untainted imaginations—meaning they still believe in the unlimited possibilities available in life. The dream is your most important ally when developing children because the dream is their motivation. The dream is the "Why." The dream can be buying a pair of Jordan's, getting a date with that cute someone in class, or going to college. Dreams are the reason kids work or steal, study or cheat. The dream is the "It."

Additionally, the dream is what helps us persevere through the tough moments in life. Millionaire businessman and trailblazer George Halsey overcame many adversities to become a wealthy business owner. When he and his wife Ruth would coach and counsel me on business, they would always talk about the importance of having a big dream to keep my momentum going. I recall George saying, "meet hard times with a harder will." I've learned when your dream is big enough and your will is unbreakable, success is imminent.

If I can find out what motivates you, then I know how to get you moving. For example you're reading this book because you have a motivating dream of helping the child you love. Allen Pease, an expert on negotiations and body language, would call that Primary Motivating Factors for reading my book.

In every situation that involves getting children to move from one place of development to the next they must be motivated by their own dream, short term and long term. We call this Dream Building. **Dream building** is the idea of not just visualizing what you want but actually going out and touching it, wearing it, driving it, walking through it...doing whatever it takes to get the desire for the thing you want so deeply inside your heart that wanting your dreams becomes needing your dreams.

A short term dream may be passing a test with a specific grade or getting an outfit, whereas a long term dream may be taking a lovely vacation or buying a house. A dream should be specific. Motivating children starts with finding specifically what they want to accomplish and what they will have by doing so. The dream should be big to them. The bigger the dream is to them the better. A space age achiever is also a space-age dreamer. Dream small, accomplish small. Dream big, accomplish bigger than you've ever imagined.

The positive results of developing a child into a Dreamer:

Children who have a big dream have accomplished 50% of the work. "The second half is implementation," as my mom would say. Children who dream big become unstoppable forces--I've witnessed this on many occasions.

One example is my dear friend and brother Samuel Welch. Sam was a country soul with a big heart, southern charm and loved to cook . His laugh was as contagious and sincere as his love. You could not help but feel love and joy when you were around him. In spite of what others thought, Samuel never let anything deter his destiny in life and he lived life on his own terms professing his faith without apology or compromise. Sam graduated from college with a business degree from Talladega College when many doubted him. He owned a profitable dessert business, loved Steve Harvey suits and sang in the choir on Sundays (it took several auditions before they let him join).

Samuel attacked his dreams with a vengeance until his untimely death. You may be wondering what's so special about him. Well, Samuel was born with an ailment that left him bound to a wheelchair his entire life. He was paralyzed from the waist down and had to live with the challenges of one who is unable to use his lower extremities.

Sam persevered through over 35 separate operations on his body before high school and many more all through his adult life. He never doubted God's ability nor did I ever hear him complain one time about anything—and he could have been justified on many occasions. Sam kept his dream at the forefront of his mind. Sam was living proof: *When the dream is big enough, the facts don't count.*

We must encourage children to stick with what they want regardless of the obstacles they face. We must push them to be unstoppable forces. Once children believe they can be greater, they will be that. When kids have the right coaching and guidance so they can see what's in their mind's eye with crystal clarity, there's nothing that can stop them. NOTHING.

Motivate children by knowing their dreams. Use those dreams to encourage children to take aggressive action and be accountable to *their* desires.

Remember the five keys to developing kids who POW:

One - Have a winning ATTITUDE. It starts with you. Believe you can help children develop his/her dreams.

Two - Teach by Doing. Be the EXAMPLE! Have some of your dreams written down first so you can share them. Your realized dreams are proof the idea works.

Three – Teach with PATIENCE. Dreams are like plants: they must grow strong roots in order to become big. Start small. Big dreams are good only once the children genuinely believe they can reach them.

Four – Teach through LOVE. Believe in their dreams and know them. Write your children's dreams on paper. Knowing children's dreams will help you hold them accountable when necessary.

Five – Have a PLAN. Make a plan to help children get a dream and chase it.

5

MAGNOLIAS, EXOTIC CARS, MANSIONS & NUNCHUCKS:

Develop Sound Work Ethics in Your Children by Fueling their Desire to Work

Make sure your level of work ethic is greater than your child's or you can forget it once they catch on to you. Photo: My father operating his coffee shop Freddies in the 80's. Pop's work ethic was relentless.

"Even so faith, if it hath not works is dead..." (James 2:14 KJV).

Developing a strong work ethic in children takes commitment, high standards and a clear vision of where the child you're developing is going. Standards must be reachable with significant effort, and the vision must be developed around your child's strengths and interests. What is work ethic? Work ethic is the amount of effort a person expresses towards a particular task or goal. Everyone has work ethic. Work ethic is scalable, which means it can be measured. So either you have a really good work ethic, modular work ethic, or your work ethic needs improvement.

The proper work ethic starts at home. No man has ***EVER*** worked me harder than my father...EVER. On the other hand, no man has taught me more valuable and useful information either. There were times when I felt that I needed to remind him that I was his son, but that would have made him work me harder.

My father has a banking, business and Real Estate background. As a young man, I had the privilege of watching him open businesses, develop office buildings and apartment complexes and negotiate deals. This is one of several reasons I decided to become a business owner. I knew that if my father—who loves me immensely, would work me so hard that I felt my eyes were crossing, how would a boss treat me?

Being financially astute, well-educated and having some knowledge of various trades were important tools for survival according to my father. They were of equal importance to him. As a result, I had very little idle time. I remember my dad always talking about how strong Banks' men are. There were times I wanted to opt for a different last name, where the kids didn't have to work so hard, but the development paid off big time!

As I stated, my father believed children should work. Therefore, if I never have another magnolia tree in my yard, I am perfectly fine with it. There's a particular house we once called home in Seattle that brings back memories. The backyard was very big and it had a deck that wrapped around the back of the house. Well, when we got the house, the yard had not been raked in a season and a half -- there was a rather large magnolia tree smack in the middle of it.

Many students are eager to learn and full of energy when they start learning the martial arts. They learn early on that good work ethics (training) are essential to being a good martial artist and leader. Children learn work ethics by watching those who lead them. Pictured: A class preparing to follow a technique I'm about to demonstrate.

His instructions were simple, “Go rake and bag the leaves in the back yard.” “Simple enough,” I thought, until I used about 40 large black trash bags. By the time I had done an average job, it was getting late in the day. I had spent the entire day raking leaves, making huge piles and trying to figure out how I could burn all the leaves and maybe even this evil tree while I was at it! Needless to say, I spent my entire weekend getting every magnolia tree leaf out the yard.

For my father, there is no exception for doing the job right and doing it exceptionally well. The same diligence that my father required me to finish the yard and do it right, he required in everything else I did, too. I could not do something halfway with him and get away with it. I was not allowed to make excuses for poor effort. I was always rewarded for hard and smart work.

My mother also carried a very high standard. My mom owned a very successful janitorial service in the Seattle area and later transitioned to education. For my sister and me, my mother impressed in our hearts and minds the idea of dreaming without limits and pressing to capture those dreams no matter the price—the cost is simply the requirement of the journey.

I can remember walking down Pike Street with my mother as a little boy, and she'd take me past this exotic car dealership.

On the showroom floor were Ferraris, Lamborghinis and other fancy cars you'll find in the Robb Report. During that time, money was very limited; in fact we didn't even own a car at the time.

Seeing those cars was inspirational to me. My mother would tell me that I can have a car like the ones on the showroom floor and I believed her. What we lacked in finances at the time, we made up for in belief. My family was and still is very rich in faith, hope and expectation. We kept our storehouse was full of big dreams.

A gentleman once said: "In the good years you put it in your pocket, but in the lean years you put it in your heart." During the lean years, my mother planted seeds of belief at a torrential rate and watered them often—she instilled hard work in us. For my mother, faith and an excellent work ethic go hand in hand.

When the mind is stretched, it never goes back. Photo: Mom, headed to an event. By this time, her business clientele included the Mayor of Seattle, lots of commercial contracts and some of the wealthiest people in the city.

My mom used various situations to get me dreaming bigger and brighter. I recall going to work with my mom and cleaning these massive houses on Mercer Island or Bellevue that overlooked Lake Washington. I was often amazed to see how affluent people were and how well they lived—I was about eight or nine years old when I first saw a swimming pool, complete with a sauna, steam room and gym on the INSIDE of someone's home. I will never forget that. My mom knew that by her children seeing more, we would strive for more. When the mind is stretched, it never goes back.

When teaching your children how to have a great work ethic, ask yourself "what kind of child do I want to produce and what kind of child do I actually have?" These are important questions which should be answered, because the answers are essential to building the right blueprint for your child's success. You may want to produce a certain characteristic in your children that frankly they don't wish to have and, as a result, miss the true gift they desire to share with the world.

So, if your kid is 7'7" and you want him to dominate on the court like Shaq, but he's more exceptional at taking apart computers-let him! His work ethic and passion toward his God-given talent will be his fuel to POW along his path in life. Plus, he will be more appreciative and receptive to the kind of relationship the both of you truly want…a strong, joyful and lasting one.

If you're having trouble developing a strong work ethic in your child, ask yourself "Am I demanding a quality or skill from my children they just don't have or care to have?" A key to giving your children an edge in life is pushing them towards THEIR PASSIONS—not yours.

Find the thing that primarily motivates your children and you have their attention. We're all motivated by something. Allen Pease calls them the Primary Motivating Factors (PMF). Here's how you find the PMF in children, ask them:

1. What do you want most? (this could be a toy, event or opportunity)
2. Why did you pick that particular thing? Why is it important to you?
3. How would you feel if you could not ever have it?
4. Why wouldn't you like the idea of never having it?

Some of you may feel this can be manipulating or bribing a child. Well, let me ask you a question: Do you go to work for peanuts or for money? If your bosses could pay you peanuts to do your job, would they? Yes, and keep more earnings for themselves! Unfortunately for the boss you're motivated by cash and not peanuts.

Children are people, not aliens. They operate on motivation just as you and I do. When children know that what they desire is within their grasps, producing a work ethic is fairly simple.

For example, I've been a martial artist since I was six years old. In Seattle, there was a martial arts supply store in Chinatown and a Hung Gar Kung Fu school above it. Talk about a piece of heaven on earth! Part of my reward for displaying great work ethic at home and at school was I could buy stuff from this store, and I could train at the Hun-gar school. This was around the time Barry Gordy's The Last Dragon hit movie theatres. The first item I bought was a pair of nunchucks! Viola, you couldn't tell me I was not Bruce

Leroy! All that was missing was "The Glow!" It was like taking candy away from a baby for my parents. Plus, my mom's favorite Chinese restaurant Tai Tung was on the same block, so it was a win-win.

Here's one more example: when I was in high school, my mom allowed me to intern at Red Zone recording studio with Tricky Stewart, Sean Hall and a bunch of other cool people. I met all kinds of celebrities and interesting people. I made an agreement with my mom to maintain honor roll status if she'd let me continue to intern. She agreed.

I would go to the studio and be there for hours and then come home, go to sleep—sometimes late in the night, get up and go to school. I was so exhausted one night working and waiting for a certain celebrity who was supposed to stop by, I had like maybe two hours of sleep when my mom made me go to school. I didn't care or put up a fuss. I had just met Toni Braxton! I felt like a lyric from a classic Kanye West song: "You couldn't tell me nothing!"

Motivating children with their dream pays big for you. Do not be afraid to step out of the box. You'll have no idea the amazing things your children can do until you allow them to do it.

Remember the five keys to developing kids who POW.

One - Have a winning attitude towards a great work ethic. Share examples of people your child admires who display a great work ethic, too.

Two - If your work ethic is poor, it may be difficult to develop an above-standard work ethic in your child. Children respond best to examples; make sure you set a good one.

Three - Work ethic takes time, especially if the children are already a little slack when it comes to work. Try to incentivize their efforts early on, but remember...patience is a key.

Four - Teach them to love working smart and working hard. Love them through the process with positive affirmations and statements of encouragement.

Five - Have a plan for building a work ethic. Children are used to things they can follow and routines. Answer some of the questions below to help you to get going.

I.R.S.

IDEAS RECOMMENDATION SOLUTIONS

DEVELOPING WORK ETHIC EXERCISE:

Jot down what rewards would motivate your child for showing improved performance in a particular area:

____

____

____

You must first recognize what you have. So, answer this question: **"What kind of child do you want to produce, and what kind of child do you have?"**

____

____

____

Be honest. These two areas must line up in order to save you from an incredible amount of frustration and your children from a great deal of irritation.

Next, determine where you want them to have a better work ethic. Sure, you can say, "Well, I want my kid to have a better work ethic overall." I understand. However, for your children to have a better work ethic overall, they must first learn to have a great work ethic one step at a time. So in what area or areas would you like to see an improved work ethic?

____

____

Is it scalable? Is there a way to mark improvement?

Once you've determined the area where you want to see the work ethic improve, you must design the scale or standards.

What are the bench marks?

What happens when they hit the mark?

What happens when they do not?

For example, if you want to see your children improve their work ethic in class, the scale may be marked by quiz grades or homework assignments—scalable. If the level of effort and understanding towards the subject is increasing, then their overall grade will increase also. There will be sufficient evidence that their work ethic has improved in this area.

By making a work ethic scalable, both you and the children can observe if there's progress, a lack of effort, or if there's a different challenge keeping you from getting the planned results. You will be afforded the ability to make the proper adjustments or seek additional help.

On a separate sheet of paper, write the scale or standards you'd like to see increased over the next week. After that, move to two weeks and then a month.

Once the scale is set, we must create buy-in. Most people do things because it makes them happy or they feel they're getting some kind of compensation for it. Just like this book, you didn't buy it because I wanted you to, you bought it because of what you hoped to get from it. Likewise, while my father set the scales and standards for a high work ethic, my mother helped create the visions and dreams to fuel it.

Have a conversation with the children in your life. Discuss the new set of expectations, the parameters, the rewards and when the change begins. A quick conversation can prevent confusion and resentment.

Remember, it's very hard to produce a work ethic if your own needs improvement. Are you striving to become the person you want your children to be? This comparison is not in terms of financial ability, education or skill. This comparison should be on a level of values and the kind of work ethic you're working to develop in your children. Remember key #2: We teach by doing. If your work ethics is sound, your children will follow you out of admiration and appreciation.

THE VILLAGE PEOPLE:

Teaching your Children to pick the Right Friendships and to maximize those Relationships!

Our C.R.O.W.N. program (Creating Righteous Outstanding Women Now) is innovating and revolutionizing the way to develop young girls with a fresh, unity-centered approach Photo: Crownin' the City in Downtown Atlanta, a "for girls only" slumber party at the Marriott Marquis. These young ladies had a ball!

Before there were cities, towns and neighborhoods there was the village. Villages were created for obvious reasons some of which were: protection, commerce and socializing. In America, the village has a more figurative connotation that reflects similar purposes along with family, support and the sharing of values.

Each of you reading this book have a village whether you know it or not. Your village is simply the people in your circle that you communicate and interact with on a regular or semi-regular basis. Your village is the people you have some sort of reliance on, and they have some sort of reliance on you. Your village may be a friend or two from work, your church, school, family and anywhere else.

One of the most important super powers you can teach a child is how to build a village and value its importance. A village provides you with a wealth of invaluable assets that stem far beyond money. A village provides resources you may not have on your own. In some cases, getting the edge can be about who you know and not what you know.

Many immigrants who enter into the U.S. know to build a village. **The foundation of a village is the idea of sticking together to accomplish common and similar goals; to pool together resources for perpetuating positive results amongst the members**.

Look around and you see different neighborhoods that may have a predominant culture or ethnicity there. In their neighborhoods they may have shops that sell familiar foods, doctors, dentist and just about every other profession available who knows how to cater to that culture.

Inside a village, as we will dissect more over the next few pages, lies a strong sense of heritage, familiarity and traditions; there's a strong sense of loyalty and camaraderie. Teaching children to build a village, teaches them how to create resources and relationships that are longstanding and beneficial. Although there are no limits to the size of your village, there should be some basic parameters when choosing to create one.

Growing up, we had a huge village. My mom would always have an extended family or several people around who teamed up with her in order for them to thrive. Our village spanned from our neighborhood to different parts of the U.S.

When I was a kid, my mom and her friends would share meals, babysit, take us out, have parties and do anything else that involved relationship-building or supporting one another. We didn't worry about not having somewhere to stay or having food. If things got tight, we'd pool our resources and thrive.

Some of my fondest memories of our village was travelling to the Indian reservations in Washington State and buying fireworks, cutting fresh Christmas trees for the holiday and mom having huge gumbo parties.

Our village was diverse. Growing up, we had friends of many cultures and ethnicities. This was a huge benefit because we were able to observe that it wasn't just our people working to make a living or facing challenges in their life. We learned just because someone shares your color doesn't mean they share your values or will support your dreams either. Consequently, we learned to judge people based on their character and not their color, religion, sexual preferences, disabilities or any other separation some people in society tend to use.

As a result, our childhood experiences were rich in adventures like road trips, trying a variety of cuisines, going to cultural festivals and anything else we could do to broaden our horizons with people.

Your Child's Village Will Resemble Your Own

In order to get the most out of the relationships, the people in your village must be equally yoked with you on whatever level you're interacting on (basically, you must be in agreement). If not, your village relationships may have negative results. Get the most out of relationships in your village. Building a better village is needed so your kids can move towards their dreams faster.

Many of us have people in our village who are either toxic or non-contributors. You know the ones, people who discourage you from accomplishing what your heart desires either through pity or by causing distractions.

Your children will model the way you develop your village. The peers in their village will be similar to the friends and kind of resourceful people (or lack thereof) you put in your village. For example, if you want wealth, your village should include some wealthy people in it. How else can you learn to be wealthy unless you have someone willing to share their secrets? Broke people cannot show you how to be wealthy.

If you want wholeness where nothing is missing and nothing is broken, you must have people in your village like that or who are at least heading in that direction. If you want Hell in your life, find people who always have drama and they'll be willing to share.

Showing your children how to develop a successful village is a key to showing them how to sustain healthy relationships. A healthy village can truly save your life. For example, the creators and directors of our C.R.O.W.N. program, Jhanai Clark and Jessica Buford, impress upon our girls the importance of teamwork, value-based relationships and respect. Our girls are a force of power and solidarity. It's amazing to watch.

There were times in my life when we did not have a home to live in. I dare not suggest we were homeless because it in no way compares to how some of our brothers and sisters have to literally sleep on the street or in worse places with their children. If not for our village (and my father), it definitely could have ended up that way.

The Right People Will Step Up From Your Village at the Right Time

Right before we moved from Seattle to Atlanta in 1992 we hit a rough patch. My mother and I stayed in a friend's small basement, sharing a small waterbed and a bathroom. Each morning we'd travel about an hour and a half to the city for school and work and then back to Tacoma. It was rough, but we always made an adventure out of these kinds of circumstances. My mother knew how to find the bright side of things for her children regardless of what she was feeling on the inside.

When we left, we shared our truck with a U.S. Special Forces Army Captain whom mom found in the newspaper want-ads. He was traveling to Fort Bragg in North Carolina. The trip took three long days.

My mom had arranged a home for us to rent on the Southside of Atlanta. After three days of driving, we unloaded a 29ft truck in a few hours, just mom and me.

Unfortunately, at that time we could not tell if the house had roaches, so after moving all our stuff—which was A LOT, the bugs began to come out of cracks and corners like they were welcoming us home from fighting a war! Worse, the roof caved in near the back room so the home was badly mildewed. You would have thought we were getting evicted the next morning at sunrise, because we packed all our stuff back on the truck and slept in it another three nights.

With nowhere to go—again, my mother called Mrs. Maywether. Mrs. Charlotte Maywether, a retired teacher my mom met when taking my sister to visit Clark Atlanta University.

Mrs. Maywether saved our lives. She put us up in her home, and helped my mother make the transition to the new city until we were able to get on our feet. Mom and I shared a room in her house. We lived there for almost two years. Mrs. Maywether's family became our family. They all helped us and we did what we could to show our deepest appreciation. Mrs. Maywether passed several years ago, but our families are still connected.

It was Mrs. Maywether who inspired my mother to become an educator. My mother educated children for 26 years in Atlanta. Imagine the lives that may not have been touched if someone in our village had not been willing to step up and assist us?

How to maneuver your village so your kids get the edge

To build your village, you must build it with people you feel support at least one of the following: your family goals, your family's interest, and your family's core values.

1. Village Members And Family Goals:

The goals of your family are the destinations your family wishes to reach as a unit in the next several months and years. Basic examples can be buying a house, adding a car, and/or taking a vacation. More advanced goals could be something like setting up college funds.

Any person you've included in your village must have respect for, and support, your family goals through action. A person who only talks, but never follows up with the coinciding action, may still be an associate, but not a person for your village. People who are willing to give towards your goals and not impede your progress are the kinds of people you want around to help you raise children. If a teacher has a co-worker or professional who can never come and do a presentation for her students after several requests—what's the point? He/she may be a great friend in other areas but cannot be considered a viable resource in terms of your village.

The professionals you bring into your village to assist with your goals must be reliable, trustworthy and committed to seeing your goals become a reality, especially if they stand to gain from them in any way. They must prove themselves faithful through action. Keep in mind, the same commitment you seek from people helping you reach your goals, you should show to them--they have goals, too. For example, if your Real Estate agent, doctor or car sales person provides great service, send them a referral or two! Far too often people only want to speak when something is wrong, but never speak out when something is going right. Make an effort to reciprocate the “love” by helping your village mates with what they’re looking to achieve. Don’t be afraid to use your resources to help someone else. Assisting each other is the purpose of the village. You all learn to Persevere Overcome and Win together.

Future NFL Hall of Fame receivers Calvin "Megatron" Johnson and Nate Burleson share a passion for helping and inspiring youth. I was honored to speak at Calvin's CJJRF workshop.

I have great relationships with many of my clients. Some of my clients have businesses or jobs that can benefit from servicing my camps, martial arts classes or other business ventures. I'm constantly looking for ways to help them, give them business or use my connections to help achieve their goals. I feel giving my clients business is the least I can do to thank them for coming back so many years to do business with me.

2. YOUR FAMILY'S INTEREST:

Family interests are things your members enjoy doing. People who assist you in this category like coaches, mentors, tutors, and instructors, often serve in other categories in your village. too. For example, your school's sports coach may also serve in your church, mosque, in your community or social circle. Many times, they serve as parent figures to many of the kids in the school.

It is imperative that the person working to develop your child has the kind of character and values you share. Kids admire and respect their coaches and instructors. This is great when you need him or her to provide an extra voice for encouragement and discipline. It's bad when they're setting the wrong example and your child follows it. What a person does in his/her home is personal until the behavior spills over to a child.

Today so many parents are looking for coaches and teachers to help their kid go pro instead of looking for the qualities which will also help their child build character and solid moral fiber. When you compromise a person of good character for Coach Idiot, the one displaying terrible habits for all to see—but can win the pee-wee trophies, your child interprets that as "I must be this way to be a winner." When the season is long over and your child is at school, whose actions get duplicated: Coach Idiot's. Guess who winds up looking like one? YOU!

Dr. Larry Moss was my high school debate and mock trial coach who instantly became a father figure, disciplinarian, mentor and, when I became an adult, friend. Dr. Moss was essential in making that possible. Not only did he carry us all over the country to compete on the national debate circuit, he was also instrumental in getting Johnny and me both full academic scholarships to the University of Alabama! Roll, Tide!

Dr. Moss was a no-nonsense kind of man. He demanded excellence from us and nothing short. He did not hesitate to put you in your place, but he also rewarded your efforts. That combination made us work tirelessly. Dr. Moss displayed solid character and expected the same from anyone around him—or you would not be around him.

One time, Johnny and I needed to get to Stanford University in Palo Alto, CA for a workshop. Dr. Moss drove us from Atlanta to Fresno, CA without taking a dime (he would have said: "you don't have any money anyway."). He dropped Johnny and me at my aunt Mary's until it was time for camp.

On the ride to California, Dr. Moss gave us the opportunity to drive. We had our permits and he was tired. There's a stretch of highway between San Antonio and El Paso that's about 500 miles long. We drove that stretch at night. That night, Johnny and I drove along listening to music; Dr. Moss was in the back sleep. We hadn't noticed we were out of gas until it was too late. All the gas stations were closed and we were in the middle of nowhere! Scared was an understatement...not of running out of gas, or the desert. We were scared out of our socks because someone had to wake up Dr. Moss and tell him the news. I believe we flipped a coin!

When we told Dr. Moss he may be stranded in the middle of Nowhere, Texas his response was simply, "You better get me somewhere, gentlemen—fast," then the guy went back to sleep! Now we were really scared while trying to find somewhere suitable to stop before the car tanked. He had NEVER been so cool—which made us really nervous.

We found a closed gas station; it was the middle of the night. I remember very vividly his facial expression when he found out that the emergency assistance company would not be able to reach us for another several hours AND they would charge him $75 for a quarter tank of gas! With a blank expression he said, "Get out." Johnny and I looked at one another and knew we'd better listen. Once we got out, Dr. Moss said "tell me when they arrive," rolled up the windows, locked the doors and went back to sleep. LOL! Luckily, I had some playing cards, so we played Tonk the rest of the night—outside on the hood of his forest green minivan.

Not only did Dr. Moss work us like we owed him money, but he loved us. He sharpened us to our competitive peaks and from there showed us how to get even better. More importantly, he taught us to believe we could compete with the best and brightest in America...we believed him and the results showed.

When developing children, there has to be a demand on the people around you to display the kind of character you want your children to have. If not, your job is harder, and you will certainly confuse your child. To a child it's simple, "If you think Mr. or Ms. X is bad, then why is he/she teaching me?" The cost of diligence is not as expensive as reversing terrible habits picked up from someone your child admires for the wrong reasons. This standard goes for anyone who deals with your children.

A family's core values are its foundation. Core values are the basic principles that your family decides to live by and make decisions under. One's values may involve faith, morality, spending habits or other principles families holds dear. Your friends, and consequently your child's friends, should share some of the same values. If I want to talk first and shoot second and you want to shoot first and talk second we will always clash. A village cannot operate in harmony unless the values line up in most areas. Of course, there are different levels to being able to walk together.

When you surround yourself with people who share your values, your children will also. Children get developed not just by you, but by the people who support you as well. If you confide in a friend to submit advice to your child and he's encouraging your child to fight which may go against your values—the mixed message will create confusion and ultimately create an undesirable result.

3. YOUR FAMILY'S CORE VALUES

A few months ago I participated in Search and Rescue (SAR) training. In SAR training, you may learn to use a Global Positioning System (GPS). During training I learned to always keep a compass handy and to never totally rely on my GPS just in case it fails me.

While out on a training assignment in the middle of the woods, my GPS battery died and I didn't have extra batteries (another mistake), Fortunately, I had a map and compass, and I had plotted my points. I used the compass to get back on track and headed in the right direction to complete the training assignment.

Your family's core values are like a compass. When in trouble or when you lose your way, your values will help you find the path to get back on track. For example, if all the people in your village share the value "stealing is bad" and they follow up with actions matching the value, the children coming from the village are less likely to steal and, if they do, the values they carry will help steer your child back in the right direction.

I.R.S.

IDEAS RECOMMENDATION SOLUTIONS

What are your core family values? If you don't have any written down, let's make some right now. Below, write 3-5 words that mean the most to you. For example you can say: The Johnson family values faith. The Johnson family values Integrity. Do not write a word but a complete sentence. This idea can be very useful when setting up a classroom also. Do them with your children; you'll be happy to see what they already value.

____

____

____

Next, briefly jot down why the words you chose have so much meaning to you. Put a date at the bottom of the page.

Congratulations! You have just created your family's (or classroom's) core values. You have given your children something to fall back on when they have character decisions to make.

Be sure to discuss their meaning and begin using them as a basis for training your children in moments of correction, redirection and praise.

BENEFITS OF A VILLAGE:

There is strength in numbers. Having a village of people who can work together solving the issues affecting children, is packed with so many wonderful and strategic rewards. Here are a few that will prove helpful almost immediately.

1. ***Support.*** Have you ever been in a crunch? If not, keep living! Having a strong support base can help you get through many situations like family deaths, layoffs, unemployment or depression. Also, they're great for helping you celebrate the high times in life, too. Having a good support system and teaching your children to do the same will enhance your quality of life. With a good support group in your village, many of life's day to-day-challenges become easier.

2. ***Discipline***. Children are less likely to have discipline problems if all the adults around them are on the same accord in terms of correcting bad behavior. It's important to agree on whatever form of discipline is acceptable in your village. Obviously, we all discipline children differently. Disciplining children was different 20 years ago. If you were at school, in the neighborhood or at a friend's house, the system of discipline was the same in many cases: you might

have gotten spanked, not only by the adult who witnessed your atrocity but then also by your parents when you got home. NOW? The water is too murky. People are getting sued, shot or thrown in jail over spanking a child.

If nothing else, a village full of people keeping an eye out and who share similar standards of what's acceptable will help keep kids in line.

3. ***Faith and Unity.*** Imagine having a village of people who pray together, praise and worship together and make an effort to adhere to the same values. Massive results are there for that group of people.

In America, look at the different cultural groups that, by moving as a single unit are making massive strides and getting supernatural results. The Hispanic community is a great example of how unity, determination, respect and single focus yield results. Of course, this is not without challenges; but in spite of the roadblocks the community is thriving.

What about the Asian and Indian communities where their people own entire neighborhoods and circulate their dollars through the neighborhood many times before it leaves? Look at Chinatowns in San Francisco and New York, Buford Highway in Atlanta and so many other places. What is it that allows these groups to thrive? Respect for each other, respect for the elderly (who are the source of wisdom), monetary progression, education, order, indomitable spirit and so much more.

One of the best forms of flattery is to duplicate. There are successful neighborhoods in America worth duplicating.

4: Camaraderie and Protection.

There is a certain comfort that comes when you know the people in your village have your back. There's also a great joy in celebrating with the people who fight alongside you. Block parties, house parties all do the same job and that's to build relationships and lasting memories with the people involved—at least that's one of the expectations.

The key to making a village is building lasting relationships which isn't always easy to do; however, it's not as hard as it may seem either. What you want to teach the children under your care is to learn how to develop win-win situations so that all parties involved feel there's a reward for the relationship. Again, the best way to show your child how to build the village is for them to watch you.

PART 2: THE CONFIDENCE CASTLE™

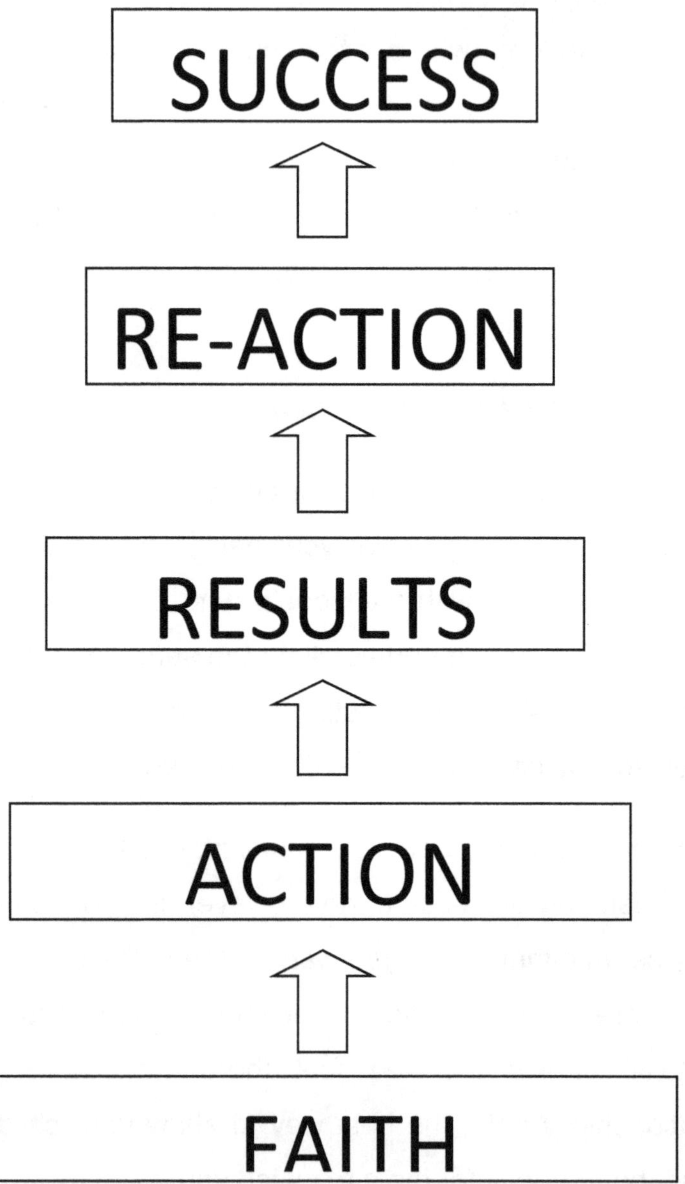

7

THE CONFIDENCE CASTLE™

Developing Unstoppable Confidence in Your Children so They Learn How to Succeed in Any Area!

Success is a decision...Success is being yourself because no one can be as successful at being you. Photo: A memorable moment was listening to Dr. Michael Eric Dyson give a presentation. In the middle of the speech, Dr. Dyson began quoting Biggie Smalls and then the audience started rapping Biggie, too! By the end, people were saying: "Dr. Dyson is so DOPE!"

What I'm about to share, I've used in each of my businesses to help children, people I work with, and myself. I have spent over two decades researching and experimenting with different strategies and the best solutions. These methods are tried and true and have been proven to work exceptionally well.

The Confidence Castle™ shows you how to build confidence in children in any area of their lives. There are five steps: Faith, Action, Results, Re-Action and Success. In every step the VTLs and the child each have responsibilities. Additionally, the VTLs have an extra responsibility of being Barriers and Lookouts which I'll explain momentarily.

According to Dictionary.com, confidence is belief in oneself and one's powers and abilities. The ability to Persevere Overcome and Win starts with children believing they can. Furthermore, children will never have the edge above their competition no matter how much time and effort you put into them if they do not believe they are worthy or capable. A level of confidence is needed to do anything, and it's one of the few character qualities that we all battle with in some area of our lives. We each have confidence and we all have different levels of confidence in every area of life. The same guy can have the confidence of Muhammad Ali when it comes to his profession but absolutely no confidence when it comes to relationships. What I'm going to show you in this chapter is how to develop a child's confidence in any area using proven principles.

As adults, our confidence is largely shaped by attitude: our experiences in life, people who took part in shaping our confidence during our formative years and the people we have *chosen* as adults to have in our lives. Children are the same way except they haven't had a ton of experiences to reference. As Village Team Leaders, we can use our experiences/knowledge to fill the gaps.

It's important that someone working with children has a positive outlook on his or her own experiences. This ensures that the perspectives one desires to duplicate will empower children to take action and not shrink back in fear.

Just because you did not accomplish a goal or dream in your personal life does not mean the same is true for the child you're helping.

Do not allow your short comings and fears to intrude on your child's dreams and desires. If your 5-year-old says she wants to be a firefighter, police officer and a fighter pilot, express belief and excitement. Anything is possible, especially with the proper timing. Hall of Fame athletes Deion Sanders and Bo Jackson both played professional baseball and professional football during a time when it was completely unheard of. A person with low confidence will find it challenging to teach a child to have confidence. They should first build their own self-image. **We must teach from the inside out: teach yourself, and then teach to children.**

8

GUARD THE HOUSE AND WATCH FOR INTRUDERS:

Village Team Leaders are the Barriers & the Lookouts!

A Barrier and Lookout must be vigilant. Stay Ready! Picture: A Camper looking out for a rabbit as the dogs flush one out.

If you've ever seen a castle or watched a movie with castles in it, you've noticed that most castles have barriers: huge walls or moats surrounding them, or there's a cliff on several sides. Normally on each corner of the castle there are lookout posts. Barriers are built to keep things out and to keep things in; safety and protection. Lookout posts were designed to see what was coming and alert the castle to prevent a surprise attack which can lead to a great misfortune.

In this example, the VTL is the barrier and the lookout. Your responsibility as a barrier is to keep all intruders out and all good stuff inside. The barrier is a way of affirming: "all that's inside belongs to me." The barrier is the one who stands between the child and his/her adversaries. You're the one who says, "Not here, not this child!" In the Bible it says: "He that hath no rule over his own spirit is like a city that is broken down and without walls" (Proverbs 25:28). Children are in the learning stages of having control of themselves. As VTLs we are the wall protecting them in hopes they will mature into citizens who "Control their own spirit." Without a wall, children are vulnerable to all sorts of attacks which is why we see so many children, especially those lacking guidance and protection, out of control today. Without a VTL, there is no one to stand in the gap for them.

We know as believers that the thief comes to kill, steal and destroy (John 10:10 KJV). A child's dreams, abilities and very breath are being attacked everyday—as ours are. Barriers help thwart these constant attacks through experience and skill. We cannot safely build a castle without a barrier. If we do, it is certain to be destroyed or worse...captured by the enemy. The barrier is there to allow time for the guards to discover motives of those wishing to gain access into the castle. A person at the gate must display great discretion and intuition.

Your job as a Lookout is to continue guiding the children through the confidence-building process and alert them to obstacles that can potentially damage or sabotage the construction process. The Lookout affirms, "I'm going to keep an eye out for all enemies human or idealistic who threaten the Confidence Castle™." As the Lookout you're using your wisdom to avoid potential dangers when possible.

In Japanese martial arts, students refer to their instructor as Sensei. The word Sensei simply means one who has gone before, or one who was born before. Either way, the implication is the Sensei has superior knowledge in the arts compared to his or her students and is therefore qualified to instruct them.

As a Lookout you are constantly looking for potential threats and administering preventative advice to the children you are serving.

As a martial arts instructor, I am always thinking of various scenarios to test my students. I am often teaching about various situations students should be aware of.

PASS THE MUSTARD...SEED

Getting Your Children Moving by Developing Their Faith!

Faith is belief in a conviction so strong, it follows with coinciding effort. Dr. C.T. Vivian exemplifies enormous faith in action. Camp Warrior King hosted the Civil Rights leader and Presidential Medal of Freedom recipient on his 92nd birthday where he spoke to our children and stressed the necessity of faith when doing what you believe is right.

Success starts with faith. To get started, a small amount of faith will suffice; the faith of a mustard seed according to the Bible (Matthew 17:20). That's extremely small. To give you an idea: a mustard seed is normally between 1-2 millimeters big. Whereas your typical black ant (the ones we normally see scurrying to grab food dropped on a picnic table are only 3.5-4.5 millimeters long! Look at it this way: a small crack in a roof is enough for water to create major damage to a structure. A small crack of faith in a child is enough to create major, positive results in his or her life.

Unwavering faith is the source fueling your child's confidence in all areas. Say this aloud please: "**Faith is the foundation, faith is the foundation…faith is the foundation.**" Everything we do can be traced back to a foundation of faith or fear. Since we were not given a spirit of fear but a spirit of power, love, sound mind, discipline and self control (2 Timothy 1:7 Amplified), our confidence and success operates on the faith foundation.

What is faith? Faith is belief in a conviction so strong that it follows with coinciding effort. This is the very reason faith can be seen.

Let's continue with the castle as an example. A castle is a massive structure and, depending on where it was built, can be seen from miles away. However, as huge as castles appear on the outside, they were designed with lower levels, cellars and dungeons that went underground—making them very dynamic and fortified from the inside out—strong foundation. The lower levels found their usefulness in daily operations and also served as reinforcement for the castle in the event of an attack of any kind. Since castles were built with a wide base they would not topple over—strong foundation.

If children were to be described as a castle, faith, one's foundation for confidence, is like their vault tucked deeply inside the castle holding the treasures and capacity of the kingdom. Faith works like a bank account: the more positive you deposit and the less you withdraw (meaning the fewer avoidable negative thoughts, experiences, word choices and people you have)—the richer you become.

In the case of developing children, a solid faith foundation means a child is receiving lots of positive deposits. This child will have a high level of self-realization, a great chance of following through on task, taking initiative and a much greater chance of achieving his or her dreams.

A weak faith foundation (great disbelief) means there are too many withdrawals causing a child to have insufficient confidence. As a result, a weak faith foundation leads to greater risk of failing on assignments, a lack of initiative and a higher propensity to have negative behavior. Worse, children with a weak faith foundation will have a much harder time realizing their potential and positively impacting their community.

Remember the five keys to developing kids who POW.

One – Have a winning ATTITUDE. Have an attitude of faith and follow that up with a level of great expectation.

Two – Teach BY Doing. Be the EXAMPLE. How is your own faith in the area you're looking to see results in children? Be sure you have, or you're working to have, the level of faith needed to complete the task. Do not have children do something you're not willing to do yourself.

Three – Teach with PATIENCE. Faith takes time to grow. Be patient and practice empathy with the child knowing his/her faith will blossom with enough watering and nurturing.

Four – Teach through LOVE. Faith improves with love. Always motivate from the positive and not from fear. So trying to motivate children by making them fear the worst is not an acceptable form of building faith—that's building fear.

Five – Have a PLAN. Have a solid plan for how you want to build a child's faith. Think about the kinds of words, phrases and visuals beforehand to improve success.

I.R.S.

IDEAS RECOMMENDATION SOLUTIONS

Ways to build your child's faith foundation

Two things a VTL can do to build children's faith: first, help them develop a winning attitude and second, help them develop a positive self-image. Bob Proctor, a well-known motivational instructor, has taught many years about the Law of Opposites (hot/cold, good/bad, etc). The theory is simply this: we can choose to think negatively or positively. Therefore, we can train our minds to find the positive in every situation.

No matter what happens, by training children to think positively in every situation, their minds now become fortified to the attacks they will face in life. Children will be more inclined to search for solutions instead of fearing the worst. Therefore, children can decide they are going to have a great day and make a new friend and their brains will seek ways to do so. Don't think so? Try it yourself.

Teach your children to control their thoughts by redirecting them as soon as possible.

A child can choose to believe they are a giant or a germ regardless of their actual size. Our thoughts, good or bad, shape our reality. For example, most of us who truly believe we are failures—are failures by definition. Why? The brain only knows to operate the program that's been uploaded by the IT department—YOU. To change how our thoughts or our children's thoughts, we must first unsubscribe to thoughts we don't want and reprogram out computers with new ideas.

For starters, we use constructive moments to develop children. This way, children will have an easier time building themselves up when we're not around. Remember, you are the voice in children's heads until they're able to formulate confident thoughts about themselves.

Second, Children must learn how to catch a negative thought once it arrives and replace the thought with a positive one. Next, children must water the new thought until it takes firm root in their mind. Once this "Rooting," process occurs, the positive thought is no longer a belief but rather a fact.

TRY THIS: (1) Right now on a piece of paper, write down how you want to feel and the things you want to accomplish each day for the next week. For example, you may say, "Today, I'm going to have an amazing day, all day no matter what or who comes my way. Nothing will stop me from having a winning attitude. I exercise each day and I will finish a book. I feel amazing because I'm meeting my goals!"

(2) Now, for the next week read the note aloud with a high amount of energy each morning, at lunch and in the evening. Make sure you read it if you have a challenging situation.

At the end of the week, reflect on how you feel. I am certain that you will feel better and your overall disposition will be better, too.

What things that can deplete the Confidence Source?

A negative thought, negative people and too many back-to-back negative experiences. The self-image is developed at home and in intimate settings like school, places of worship and extra-curricular activities. All too often, these places serve as breeding grounds for negativity and image destruction.

To combat the negative attacks, children must have a fresh series of victories in their minds at all times. It's hard for anyone to believe they can finish a marathon if they can never even recall finishing a lap.

Question: How many oranges can you pick from an apple tree?

VTL's have several responsibilities when developing children's faith. The first and foremost is to **plant the seeds of the results you desire. You cannot get oranges from an apple tree!**

In my martial arts and self-defense program one of the things we teach children from their first day in class is the I AM Creed. The I AM Creed is a series of affirmations the children say EVERY time we have instruction...EVERY TIME, with deep conviction. Why? I want my students to hear themselves say these powerful words so much that they believe them.

I know that words are seeds, so by them saying the I AM Creed in every class, the children are watering their seeds and it works like crazy!

I am building their faith by planting positive words that my students can use in any area of their life. I use these phrases to encourage effort. As I said earlier: You will have what you say!

Encouraging effort is essential to building confidence because effort takes goals from the imaginary realm to the physical realm. In a beginner's martial arts class for example, I may demonstrate a front kick or reverse punch—which is usually followed by a "Whoa!" or "awesome!" from the new children in class. I want my children to know that what I'm telling them to do is possible (remember, we teach by doing). Next, I may say, "How many of you think you can do this?" At this point some kids are extremely excited and some are not. To the ones who are lacking confidence I may respond with a positive affirmation like "I'm sure you can do it if you put forth a little effort."

Sometimes, I may have a group of kids who are scared to try an exercise, and I normally instruct them to see themselves doing a front kick or punch in their mind first (imaginary realm). The key is building their urge to try. As a VTL we not only want our children to believe they can achieve, but we want kids to believe so hard that they'll just burst if they don't have a chance to act on their belief! When you ask children "Hey you think you can do 'it?" and they respond with "yes," they're ready.

Once we've started promoting effort in children we must **continue to water the seed** through suggestions on how to take action coupled with positive affirmations until the children are ready to act. True belief has not been built if students are not willing to try. In time, if the foundation is built correctly, operating in faith will become involuntary. They will breathe in faith and exhale confidence. But for now, let's get them believing.

Persevere Overcome Win!

Let's do a quick recap of the VTL's duty in building faith, the Confidence Source:

- Plant seeds of the desired result
- Promote Effort
- Continue to water the seeds.
- Remember faith is the foundation, not fear.

10

DON'T GIVE THEM TIME TO BE AFRAID:

Beating F.E.A.R. by Getting Your Child to Take Action Fast!

It's important to get children acting skillfully before they can ponder over their F.E.A.R. Photo: One of my young female students executing a front kick with precision timing against a male sparring partner. There's an unfortunate misconception in society that females lack enough skill and strength to defend themselves against male fighters...my girls seem to do just fine.

Action cures fear. The very act of doing or pressing through what you fear creates a sense of confidence through accomplishment. Take a person afraid of flying for example. When they first step on the plane and even before they arrive at the airport, there may be illusions of the plane going up in flames or some catastrophe. However, once they take a flight and come back safely, a piece of the fear is gone. As that person continues to fly, more and more pieces of fear fall off until it becomes second nature to get on a plane to travel.

Action creates **power** and power by definition is *the ability to get results*. Fear on the other hand is best used as an acronym meaning **F**alse **E**vidences **A**ppearing **R**eal (F.E.A.R.). This means, the negative thing or situation we perceive may happen to us is usually all in our heads.

As a VTL, when we get children to act, we have now instilled in a child the ability to get results over **F**alse **E**vidences **A**ppearing **R**eal! You now have an empowered child on your hands who can overcome his/her fears! Watch out, world!

In my martial arts classes I may say, "Ok, let's do ten front kicks together, ready?!" And without giving them the time to ponder the notion, together we start kicking and kihaping (yelling—something kids love to do). Also, if we do one side, then we must do the other. Now, what did I just do? I just brought the imaginary realm (faith or belief) to the physical realm, I've built some belief in the students because they're kicking (technique is irrelevant at this point) and I got the kids to do twenty kicks instead of ten…I continued to plant the seeds of faith and confidence…powerful stuff.

Furthermore, actions produce outcomes which gives us, the VTL's, something to correct, teach and guide. Once children act, we have their attention… if only for the moment.

Your job in the action stage is **to promote more action (**the more action the more belief is created), praise and promote (remember, we continue to water the seeds i.e.: "Wow, that's a good job!") and look for opportunities to move them to the next stage in the Confidence Castle.

Remember the five keys to developing kids who POW.

Your perspective at this stage should be focused on the action itself, not how well the action was executed. We can fix the techniques later. Some action is better than no action at all. Your level of excitement should be high, especially if the child expressed deep fears in attempting the act.

Encourage action by showing an example or several if needed. So, if you want a child to jump out of a plane, guess who has to jump first? Bingo, the one with all the lingo! YOU!

Kids are fast learners. They enjoy fun, exciting challenges. Don't be afraid to pour out information and require a lot of action. Kids can handle it. By the end of a class, you know you've got it right when you've inspired zeal for learning. Picture: Zeal from a great group of kids...and a hungry instructor! Lunch was so good. The staff fed me well, LOL!

Do not force a child to act until he/she is ready. The child must be willing. Patience is the key. It will take some children many tries at bat before they actually swing. Sometimes, we must even alter our approach or equipment to get a kid to act.

As part of our development program we participate in what's called a Hunt and Learn. In a Hunt and Learn we teach children how to hunt wild game using rifles and or shotguns depending on the hunt. In our programs we hunt deer, rabbit, squirrel, turkey and quall depending on the season. One time at a hunt and learn, we had a student named Tony who was deathly afraid of the sound shotguns made when discharged.

As a safety measure, all students must practice shooting before we hunt, and he was the last one to practice. Tony's father had made an investment for the weekend and started to get frustrated with his son's very apparent fear.

Since this was a squirrel hunt, we wanted the kids to hunt using .410 shotguns which is the smallest size shotgun in terms of round size—perfect for kids, yet the blast was too loud for Tony. With time running out, we made an adjustment to a small .22 rifle which has virtually no sound but requires a better aim and bull's eye! Tony overcame his fear, shot the rifle and was ready to hunt.

Important points to remember about Action:

<u>Action:</u>

- Action cures fear
- Action builds belief and attacks disbelief
- Action creates measurable outcomes
- After initial action, VTL's should promote more action and look for ways to move the child to the next level

Action builds big-time belief and primes the child for more difficult stages in life.

11

MISTAKES, THE SECRET SAUCE TO SUCCESS:

Successfully Analyze the Results & Find Silver Linings!

"When the dream is big enough, the facts don't count."--Dexter Yager. One of many powerful things I learned from Dexter is how important it is to make your time count. You must have some quantifiable result that gets you closer to your goal each day.

I've had the opportunity to learn from, model and spend time with a lot of trail blazers. Dexter Yager is recognized by many people around the world as a business icon, success teacher and innovator. One of the many principles that sticks in my mind from Dexter's teachings is his philosophy on results. Dexter would say, "Results, results, results, results, I am out to create RESULTS!" in reference to Dexter making sure he got positive outcomes from every business meeting.

I believe that same attitude and determination must be used here in reference to children. When we're attempting to increase a child's confidence, our next step is to review the results. We want the kids to create results, and action gives us results.

Results are important because when results are happening, excitement is created. When excitement is created, it's much easier to correct and redirect a child's efforts. Excitement can nitro boost one's motivation better than just about anything. An excited child will push further, faster, harder and stronger. ZOOM, ZOOM, BABY!

In this stage we carefully analyze results and determine the correct actions to take. By analyzing the results and learning from the mistakes, you will find the clues to success.

The VTL should ask questions like: what were the outcomes to the actions? Is the child producing the outcome I'm looking for? If not, how can we modify the inaccuracies? Write them down. These questions will guide you and help you to best assist the child.

During the results stage, it is important to keep the proper perspective. What may appear to be bad is actually good if you look deeper. The right or wrong action is irrelevant when considering the child you're assisting has just increased his or her confidence enough to take action.

As long as the child remains excited and willing to put forth effort, you can make adjustments until you get the outcomes you desire. Keeping the right perspective is a key to producing change.

How to handle results:

- Find the results! Remember action creates results. Look around and find them. They are there!
- Analyze and ask questions.
- Make adjustments. Begin to move the child towards the desired level of confidence needed to accomplish the task.
- Find the silver lining. What may look bad can be viewed from a different perspective. Find it. The right perspective may save you some time.

12

GROUNDHOG DAY:

Getting Your Child Acting Again and Again Until Its Right!

Accomplishing any task requires a level of discipline equal to the size of the task. Doing the same thing repetitively requires discipline and is necessary to become proficient at almost anything. In this picture, students are working to improve their fighting stance.

It's nearly impossible to see marked improvement without using repetition. Therefore, it is critical for children to execute the task you're looking to improve once they've started trying. You must implement **Re-Action.**

Re-Action is encouraging and convincing the child to act again and again after you have reviewed and corrected the outcomes together. Think player-coach relationship: The player executes a technique, the coach discusses how to do it better, and the player executes the technique again and again using the corrections until the player displays a level of proficiency satisfactory to the coach. The Village Team Leader **encourages the correct re-action based on the results**. Confidence, like faith, can be seen. Children, who act, are corrected and execute the correct action repetitively, show big signs of growing confidence and discipline. Children who go through the Re-Action process will show confidence in themselves and express a great deal of confidence in your leadership and knowledge.

Note: **not all children will display their confidence the same**. Some kids are outgoing and others are reserved. To miss this concept is to miss the whole lesson. **It's not as important that you see the massive change you desire compared to the child seeing who he/she is becoming in the process of developing greater confidence through repetition and improvement**.

In regards to re-action, remember to analyze the journey. Where are they now, compared to when they first started? For example, if a journey starts where a child is just trying to gain enough confidence to enter gymnastics and now she's inside the gym and ready to tumble...Great job, you have marked improvement and more importantly, a more confident child!

The re-action and results phases will take the longest to get through when building the Confidence Castle. You and your child may go through the re-action to results cycle many times before you move to the next section in the diagram.

NFL Hall of Fame player and Coach Tony Dungy put it this way: “It's the journey that matters; learning is more important than the test. Practice well and the games will take care of themselves.”

How to implement the Re-Action stage:

- Encourage the correct action based on the results. Continue to build faith and to analyze the results. Correct the wrong actions. Repeat this step as many times as needed.
- Children express confidence differently. Don't give up just because children may not “Appear confident” to you. Be sure to ask how they feel. Trust their response.
- What children see in themselves matters most. As a VTL, help point out moments of progress where they can notice the growth, too.

13

THE NEVER-ENDING JOURNEY:

Getting Your Child to Succeed and Attain Multiple Successes After!

Once a child experiences success, savor the feeling for a moment and MOVE ON so that the momentum of the success-confidence cycle is transferred to other areas of his/her life. Photo: a group of exhilarated campers tackling some wild rapids. We wanted them to see that confidence can be transferred into multiple areas—especially the unknown areas.

To build confidence we must build successes. Recall the last time you accomplished something big? Do you remember the rush, the pride? Do you recall winning something and afterwards feeling invincible or unstoppable? Have you ever had that moment when you said, "I'm the best?" Didn't that feeling carry you for a moment? Children are the same. How do children act when they finally pass a test they feared they'd fail? How do child athletes respond when they hit a homerun at a baseball game?

When children experience success, their confidence increases and when their confidence increases so does the amount of success they have in other areas as well. I call this the **Success-Confidence Cycle.** Simply put, the more you win, the more you believe; the more you believe, the more you win. The two concepts thrive on each other like a beautiful marriage.

The Success-Confidence Cycle is very contagious, too. Have you ever watched a sports game on TV and noticed that when a particular player makes a great play, he/she runs to teammates and to share their success with high fives and celebrations? Next are series of successes, the entire team morale changes! That's because a winner can inspire other people to be winners, too.

The success experience is very tricky. I call it an experience and not a level because it can be like a slippery slope. Success, as described by famed motivator Dr. Earl Nightingale, "Success is the progressive realization of a worthwhile dream or goal." That means success is on-going, forever a journey...not a destination. The moment we start believing we've "arrived" at success—that's normally when we can expect to begin heading backwards.

Once a child has success with an objective and has a taste of great confidence, it is important to celebrate, savor the feeling for a moment and MOVE ON so that the momentum of the success-confidence cycle is transferred to other areas of his/her life. It's like getting a power-up in a video game where the characters become invincible for a moment! What else can they tackle? What other games, tasks or hobbies can they excel at or do?

When kids I'm training have success, I want them moving on and having torrential moments of enlightenment in as many areas as possible. I'm like a scout looking for other areas they can conquer with their new super-power. As a Lookout, make sure you are seeking out new areas to conquer with this new confidence.

On the other hand, we have the **Failure-Doubt Cycle**: the more we fail the more we doubt. In a game where a team is getting beaten really badly, as in basketball when a team goes on a 10-0 scoring run, the coach may call a timeout to regroup his or her team and build the morale back up.

Great coaches know that if they don't break the momentum of failures, their players' morale may get so low that winning the game will get out of reach.

When your children are experiencing a series of failures, call a timeout, pump them with positivity until you see the spark back in their eyes, and put them back in the game!

Additionally, enlightenment in many circumstances can be superior in some ways when building confidence. Yes, I can show you how to do something, but it's still mine because I showed you. In contrast, if I give you just enough that you can stumble upon new ideas yourself through practice, now you own it because you have earned the lesson through trial and error.

Once children "own" their confidence, no one can take it away. They will always have a point of reference if they lose their way--like using a map and compass.

Remember the five keys to developing kids who P.O.W.

Your attitude toward success is simple: Make it a big deal. Success is not easy to come by. Also, this motivates a child to push hard at the next objective. You want a series of victories not just one.

Persevere Overcome Win!

It's important to share moments when you've had successes in life. Be sure to share how you felt and use it as motivation for the child.

Every child will handle success differently. Some may relish in the moment too much and others may not feel they're worthy. Be patient so you can identify the differences and handle accordingly.

Celebrate with the children. When they succeed, you also have a significant part in their success.

Have a plan of action for after the success. Where do we go from here?

I.R.S.

IDEAS RECOMMENDATION SOLUTIONS

Keys to remember on the Success Stage:

- To build confidence, we must build successes.
- As the Lookout, praise and promote, then keep the children moving from one success to another success. Look for other areas where they can win.
- Children lacking confidence may need to enjoy their winning moment longer; be sure to help them recall their wins when needed.
- Avoid prolonged moments in the Failure-doubt cycle. Stay here too long, and the faith foundation will erode. Keep positive momentum at all cost; it's hard to gain it back.
- Self-enlightenment is critical. When children can recognize they've succeeded or amassed knowledge through effort and a willingness to dig deeper for results, they have a greater sense of self-efficacy.

- Success is not a destination but a journey or a stop along a bigger journey called life. Once a castle is built in one area we must move on to another.

The Confidence Castle™ is a series of cycles. Children should be moved to the next level once you believe they have an understanding of the concept. Since building confidence requires progression, holding a child at a level for too long may have the reverse effect of what you're seeking.

Remember, children have increased their confidence once they decide to try.

The process of building confidence is getting children to see where they've come from and who they're becoming. We all battle with our self-esteem in one way or another. Most children have enormous amounts of confidence and just don't know it. Your job is to help them see it.

Dexter Yager puts it this way, "Real confidence comes from winning and losing enough that you know the difference, so that every time you lose, you're only stumbling forward to win again."

14

HEAR YE, HEAR YE:

How to Keep the Castle Built!

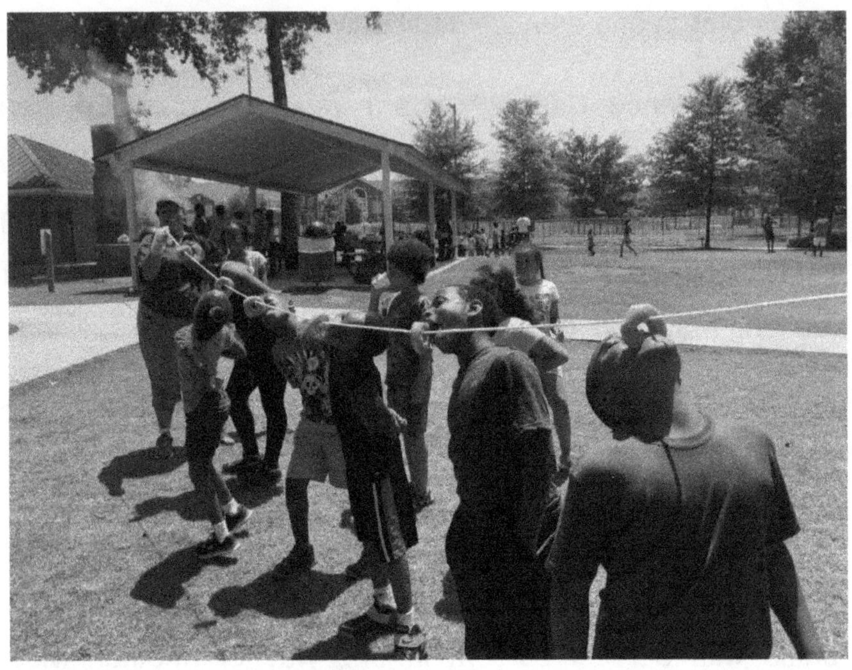

PLANT POSITIVITY! Pictured: A moment when you want to be a kid again...

HEAR ME: IT ALL STARTS WITH YOU! Your voice, good or bad, eventually becomes the voice in your child's head. Be positive. Here are a few phrases you can use every day to boost self-confidence:

- I believe in you!
- I know you can do it!

- You know, you've got what it takes!
- I'm so proud of you!
- Good job!

Being positive NEVER gets old. Every opportunity you get to plant seeds of positivity—TAKE IT! Create small successes for your child by celebrating an achievement each day no matter how small. Don't forget, you're trying to build confidence. Give a nice gesture, a high five, a sticker or bring home a favorite dessert or meal.

Here are examples of a few small successes you can use to build your children's confidence. Simply acknowledging your children do well when they are:

- Taking initiative on hygiene practices
- Making the bed; cleaning the bedroom
- Doing homework without being told
- Doing chores without being told
- Keeping silent and not talking back disrespectfully
- Reading a book without being prompted

Once your children begin to do the things you're looking for, it's paramount to give them recognition—consistently--until it becomes second nature. The praise-for-effort system works great for kids of all ages. Recognition… it's what babies cry for, men die for.

Edify, edify, edify…edify, edify, edify…

I cannot express the importance of genuine edification enough. In my experience, when you sincerely edify someone, you're creating a special moment that leaves a positive impact. This is a HUGE DEAL, especially with children. Don't you just love being recognized for your hard work and efforts--especially in front of others? Genuine edification is one of the best ways to express appreciation and without question one of the best ways to build confidence.

When you edify children, build them up IN FRONT OF OTHERS! That is the key with this next exercise.

For the next 30 days take selective opportunities to edify your child when you're within earshot of strangers. It will be like pouring fuel on to their "fire." Take opportunities to edify your child in front of people: at family gatherings, school functions, public places and any other location where people may be around! I challenge you to go for it!

The key is to be genuine and focus on praising performance and/or behavior. Why? First, we don't want to build conceit in a child. Second, the performance and/or behavior the child is displaying we want to continue. Third, some children have a hard time believing good things about themselves, but will find it difficult to deny their own efforts.

Through your genuine praise, the voice inside your children's heads will grow louder and louder with positive thoughts about themselves. After a while, with enough love and complements, your children will begin to edify their positive performances and behavior on their own. Watch out, ladies and gentlemen, here comes a superhero!

Note: some children absolutely DO NOT like to be praised in front of others...they may find it embarrassing. It's import to be aware of this feeling and respond accordingly. Genuine edification without on-lookers will work just as well for these children. It's also important to note that not all children like verbal edification. Edification can be done through non-verbal communication like a gift for performance, spending quality time doing their favorite activity and more.

Parent-Projected Negativity: the Coup

I'm sure you've seen someone humiliate his/her child in public (but I know you would never do this). Isn't it terrible—some enraged adult's fangs, horns and tail coming out on a smaller—usually guilty child or adolescent? What's worse is the adult is normally upset about a totally unrelated issue but decides to use his/her power on the ones they have control over.

Humiliating your child in public especially about a private matter very rarely yields the result you're looking for. It's embarrassing, and you'll regret it in the long run. Don't do it.

Building self-confidence is not something that can be accomplished overnight. It is a process that improves with positive experiences and being surrounded with the right people. Building Confidence is like bathing: It's noticeable when you do it regularly and when you don't.

15

SUPERGLUE:

Six Ways to keep your child in a winning state of mind and AWAY from depression!

Tony Robbins, one of the greatest and most widely-recognized motivators on the planet. Tony often speaks on the importance of being in the right mental state. I believe if you can master your state, you have gotten that much closer to mastering self. Children need this tool.

Children must learn how to keep themselves in a winning state of mind and out of mental moments that lead them down a toxic road. Having a winning state of mind is something that must be practiced until it becomes a serious habit. Furthermore, having a winning attitude does not mean you won't experience negative situations or outcomes, but rather you know how to combat them and get back into a positive state as quickly as possible. Persevering Overcoming and Winning is rooted in the ability to constantly see the glass half full even when others feel otherwise.

Research shows for every one negative experience children have in a day; they need five positive ones to off-set the one and get back to a positive state. What's also important is that the children are able to attack the negatives quickly and not allow them to fester.

Child experience negative and positive situations through the same senses (hearing, seeing, feeling, etc). This is a clue for keeping children in a winning state. We make sure the children are receiving more positive experiences than negative ones through their senses each day.

Keeping a child in a winning mental state means more than taking in positive when faced with negative; it's flooding the mind with positive often so that the mind is fortified with positivity and able to swiftly defeat any negative attacks.

Here are six proven and effective strategies that are sure to pull your child out of an emotionally paralyzing state and back into a winning attitude. No strategy carries more weight than the other, and I recommend using a variation of solutions. No two children are the same, so the VTL should determine which combination of solutions works best.

1. **Teach your children to give themselves motivational pep talks aloud.**

For some odd reason, people have been taught it's bad to talk to yourself and provide an answer. I don't know about you, but I tend to have conversations with myself all the time, especially when I'm engaged in a project. Most of the leaders and successful people I know do the same thing. We call it thinking.

Frankly, I believe people should talk to themselves more often—especially in a motivational sense. Children are no different. Saying positive affirmations aloud and giving the "before the big game speech," is an effective way for a child to combat the negative things people say.

Positive self-affirmations force a child to develop a stronger mental state. It requires a particular amount of will-power to negate a bunch of negative clutter in the mind. Phrases like: "you are smart," "Ignore the negative opinions of others," "it's ok, just try harder next time," will create a sense of reprieve for a child.

Teach your children to talk to themselves by giving them the right things to say to themselves when something good or bad happens. When something happens ask them, "What did you think when (Blank) happened?"

List 3 positive phrases your child may begin using now:

____

____

____

2. **Teach your children to listen to positive music or motivating talks.**

Ever see sports players wearing headphones before a game? Ever wonder what kind of music they're listening to? Chances are it's something that's putting them into a winning state of mind. Listening to something positive is a great way to change your mental state. Nowadays there are all sorts of playlists that cater to your mood. What's even more effective are audios of speeches and presentations that focus solely on motivating people. I know, many children may not have the attention span to listen to a 45-minute talk of Les Brown, but I tell you a 3-minute one may do the trick.

Here's the reality: the positive audio your children listen to can be an audio of your voice saying positive things to them. It can go right on the $500 smart phone they have, too. Don't make this complicated. Just do it!

Suggestion: Make a playlist of motivating songs your children may like to hear when they're having a rough day.

Find or make a short 5-minute or less audio of yourself or an excerpt from a motivational speaker that will be sure to pump up your kid.

3. Teach your children to watch something motivating.

I recently taught a lesson at our Fall Family Extravaganza where I asked the audience what movies would be motivating to watch if they're having a bad day. There were some very interesting answers, but the one that struck a chord was the mom who shouted out, "Rocky!" She has the right idea.

Watching something motivating on media is not only a powerful way to help you push forward, but an extremely effective way to get your mind off of a troublesome issue. The more relatable the media the child is viewing, the greater the impact. Aspiring athletes, after watching their favorite player on TV, may go outside afterwards and practice because they've been motivated by what they saw.

Visuals are very powerful. The next time you want to turn up the fire on your children, find something that relates to their passion and have them watch it.

List 3 movies your kids love that will get them motivated.

____

____

____

4.**Teach your children to read something motivating that relates to their situation.**

Very few things can capture our attention like reading something motivating or positive especially when we're faced with a crisis. Many children are swamped with stinking thinking and have negative perspectives out of habit. Reading changes the way we think about things and, as result, changes our behaviors and actions. The next time your children have a challenging situation, have them read something relatable that will help pull them out of the slump.

List three books your children can read for positive reinforcement:

____

____

____

5: Teach your children to talk to someone who knows how to uplift them specifically:

Sometimes we all just want to talk to a person who understands or can help us process a situation. When teaching children how to pull themselves from an emotional slump, it's important they have the right kinds of people to talk to. The right person can set them on fire to take charge and press through their situation. The wrong person can make matters worse.

List 3 People your children can call when they face a challenge:

____

____

____

#6 Teach your children to help someone

Photo: A group of our teens packing boxes at the Atlanta Food Bank.

Helping someone in need is a great way to take the attention off of yourself, and also helps you put things back into perspective. Uplifting children who truly appreciate the assistance, will make them feel better. It might even help them through their challenges. Helping others has stress releasing powers.

List three people or organizations you and your children can help:

____

____

____

Now that you have the six ways to keep your children in a winning state of mind, try them all first and see which ones your children respond to best. Once you have the answers, teach your children to use them to help them Persevere Overcome and Win through their challenges!

16

START THIS CONVERSATION EARLY:

Teaching your Children the Four Basic Pillars of Financial Literacy!

Banker and Financial Specialist Rich L. had our campers talking and thinking like real money experts at our financial literacy classes. Not only did our kids learn a great deal, they had a blast, too!

Financial literacy and money management should be discussed more in the home and taught in schools. I believe many families don't discuss the topic for several reasons: families feel the money topic is complicated, talking about money can be stressful, money talk is boring, or the adult feels he or she lacks financial literacy themselves.

As an adult, you are already knowledgeable enough to teach basic money principles with your children. The key to teaching about money to children is to keep it on a level they can understand. The principles of money are similar to other basic principles in life. This chapter is going to show you the parallels between financial literacy and some of the principles of life so that you can teach the concept of money much more easily to the kids you love.

I am no financial planner or accountant, but I'm sure most financial professionals would agree that money management and financial literacy is all about becoming knowledgeable about money and applying that knowledge.

It's been said that money is simply a tool that's used to buy goods and services. Some tool, huh? On the contrary, it's also been said that money isn't everything, but it is right up there with oxygen—you gotta have it. I agree with both analogies.

It is NEVER too early to start teaching children about money, and it's NEVER too late. It doesn't take long to have the conversations either. How long does it take to say, "Kid, don't spend all your money, save some, invest some." I know that doesn't sound fancy, but if you ever talk to a financial professional, they basically say the same thing.

The concept that's required and takes more discipline from the VTL is a big word called CONSISTENCY. When educating children about money (or anything else for that matter), YOU MUST BE CONSISTENT! Don't stop talking to them about being smart with their money. My dad has talked to me about money since I can recall, and he still slips in conversations about money today. Of course, the conversations have become more complex. Talking to children about money early is essential and will give them a huge edge over their friends down the road.

The Stones, a family I admire and have developed a strong relationship with over the years, talks with their son regularly about the family's monthly budget, where the money in the home goes, and the cost of buying certain items in their house. They've been educating their son Michael this way since he was able to understand the concepts. As a result, Michael has a great understanding of how money works, how to be smart with money, and how to use it.

Some families are embarrassed to discuss money matters with their children yet get upset when their kid comes and asks for a $250 pair of shoes. "What, you think money grows on trees?!" The answer to that question is, they don't know or won't really care unless you educate them on how money works.

There are four basic pillars you should be discussing with your children in relation to money. These principles should be taught first in the home, but since that's not possible for every child, I've made them easy to teach by anyone. The four pillars of financial literacy are:

Pillar #1: Teaching Kids to make money

Pillar #2: Teaching Kids to save money

Pillar #3: Teaching Kids to Invest money

Pillar #4: Teaching Kids to Leverage money

PILLAR #1 TEACHING KIDS TO MAKE MONEY:

When teaching about money, its important to teach about service. Providing a needed service gives back more value than just money. In this picture, one of our campers is ready for a call, during one of our annual Service Appreciation Days!

I don't recall my father ever just giving me money. I do recall him teaching me all kinds of financial skills and giving me many ideas to make lots of money. As a kid, my father required that I also read the business section of the newspaper EVERYDAY so that I could learn about how other successful people were making money, how businesses work, and understand the concept of investing. As an adult, it became a habit to continue to learn about money. Pop would say, "How would you look being broke with a last name like Banks?"

Some of you may or may not have the banking and business background my father has, but you do have experiences with money that will benefit the children you love. Share those experiences and what you've learned from them. It's important to share those experiences before your children come to you with a mistake you could have prevented with a 10-minute conversation. Give your children the chance to make a better decision because they hear your voice in their heads. I can personally attest to hearing my parents giving me insight about a situation and then being in that very situation and hearing their voices. It has saved me many times, and it will save your children, too!

The Bible says, "Direct a child in the way he should go and when he is older, he will not depart from it." (Proverbs 22:6)

You don't have to be a financial advisor to educate children about money or how to make it.

Children need to learn how to make money early on. It will teach them to appreciate having money, expand their creative minds and improve critical thinking skills. Since money, or the need for it, isn't something we can avoid, you might as well teach your children to be as financially successful as possible.

Money, as we stated earlier, is used to buy goods and services. That means money can be made by providing goods and/or services, too. Everything we tend to buy is either a good (a thing) or a service (something people provide to you or on your behalf). Find what people want or need and you have a means of making money. It's really that simple.

So, depending on the age, when you're attempting to teach your children how to make money, instead of giving money when asked, suggest the children develop a creative way to earn it. What do I mean by that? Am I saying that when your kids want a toy, I should make them earn it instead of just going out and buying it?" Yes, and here's why: Is the toy free? No, what about the gas to get there and the time it takes? Point is when you're teaching children about how to make money, when they earn the money, children value the rewards more and they are less likely to be careless. The entire process opens up conversations that create immense education potential.

One way to prevent your kids from having a habit of wasting is to make them earn more of what they have. Friends will be less likely to destroy or mistreat the things your children learn to value. Again, earning an item gives it greater value.

Children should not earn money for things they're to do anyway like chores. If a kid wants five bucks for making his bed, yeah right; five bucks for moving some old boxes out the garage, deal! When teaching a kid to make money, you teach work ethic. Your children will never be broke because early on they'll know: "If I want to make money, I must think of a need and fill it." This principle will carry on throughout their lives.

I remember when my father first taught me how to paint. I was about eight or nine, and I learned by painting one of the units in a building he owned. I remember it being a lot of fun, and I had no idea how valuable that "class" would be. Later on as a teenager, I'd make extra money painting (in addition to other skills I acquired). From that time, there have been many cases in my life where I saved a lot of money and made money because I learned how to paint. There were also times, where I was able to keep a roof over my head, because of those skills.

Teaching children to make money allows them to be more self-reliant. They will always look for ways to create income. Long term, a child who knows how to find creative ways to make money will always be able to generate it.

My team and I have recently started a program called the Exceptional Kid Campaign (EKC). The EKC is a program designed to find children who are doing exceptionally well at extra-curricular activities while getting good grades. Some of my favorite interviews are the ones with children who have built businesses. There's something different about a young boy or girl who has to find a need, develop a plan, and execute an idea. The amount of skill, patience and fortitude it takes to do that is truly special.

Remember the five keys to developing kids who POW.

What is your own attitude towards money? Your attitude towards money will influence the children you're helping. If you're not sure of your perspective, take a few minutes to decide on one before you teach.

If you plan to teach children how to make money, you should probably be doing so yourself. Remember we teach by doing.

Not every child will have the discipline to be a business owner. This is OK. Most children want things and, therefore, are motivated to at least work for these things to some degree. It will take time for some children to understand money is earned and not given. Be patient.

Remember to love the children through their mistakes; their mistakes are where they may have the most valuable lessons.

Have a plan for teaching a child to make money. Look below for some great ideas.

I.R.S.

IDEAS RECOMMENDATION SOLUTIONS

Steps to teaching children to make money:

1. **Find their interest, dream or goal.** Why do your children want to make money? It can be as simple as a favorite toy or video game to as big as saving for a car.

   It's best to build a business centered in something your children are seriously interested in. People are more likely to excel financially in areas where they have an interest.

When I was a kid, I wanted to make money, and I enjoyed being outside, so I came up with all kinds of creative, legal ways of doing it. I did not care. I would walk dogs; rake leaves, clean out garages, cut grass, whatever.

2. **Find a need.** One of the basic principles in economics is Supply and Demand. If you can match what people are demanding with the right product or service and the right amount, you will make money.

3. **Develop a plan.** It is crucial that you AND the children come up with a "business plan." This should be a simple: Who, what, when, where, how and why. Nothing too complicated—they're kids. Write the idea on a piece of paper. If you have time, create a business agreement. The idea is: as long as the children are having fun in the process and starting to make money then do what comes to mind.

4. **Get to work.** It's important to get started fast. Don't take too long. You want to emphasize that making money is easy to do and simple to execute. If you

take too long, you'll lose their attention. With the right idea, you and your children can start a business and start selling in a few hours or less.

Here are two brief examples:

(1) Younger children can have a business where they provide a service for their home. Something like a shoe organizing business where they organize their parent's shoes each week for a fee. This business is very basic but could be a lucrative start for a young kid and fills the need for a less-motivated parent.

(2) A mobile car-wash business. This will work really well for a kid in a subdivision or apartment complex. Buy a basic handheld vacuum, some other basic supplies and you're in business. Use the neighbors' water—they won't mind, they're saving money, trust me. If your kids are good, they're in big business.

A family we recently interviewed helped their young boys start a business making bracelets. The boys are learning about supply and demand, profit and loss, and all sorts of business principles in addition to saving for college and having video game money.

By teaching your children to make money at a young age, you provide them with an edge to making money later in life.

Your children will be able to overcome the demands of making a living by being able to generate dollars and opportunities when others are waiting in line trying to find a job.

So, make it fun, and remember the adage: Keep It Simple, Superhero!

PILLAR #2 TEACHING KIDS TO SAVE MONEY

What can be better than making money? Making more money, of course, and saving some of what you make. So now that we've taught our kids to make money, we have to teach them to hold on to some of it. This step can become increasingly difficult to do the longer you wait to start—but it's never too late.

Saving money is simply a matter of creating the habit. Now, habits we all know are harder at first and when done long enough become second nature. It's the same with money. Saving money enables you to have peace of mind, having options and, more importantly, being able to capitalize on opportunities.

Saving money is crucial to Persevering Overcoming and Winning. It will be much easier to deal with a rough patch in life when you face it with some sort of reserve.

There's always a question of how much to save. That's up to you and the kids to decide based on the goals you create. I believe that what's more important than the actual percentage is actually getting children into the habit of saving money. You can always make adjustments later. Get them saving now!

When I was a kid, one time I made $100 raking some lawns, so I decided to buy myself a telephone for my room that was made like a Harley motorcycle. Yes, this was back when homes had landlines and no cell phones. My parents would get pissed tripping over those long cords headed to my room to take the phone away. Anyway, the phone was $90. When my dad found out, he made me put the phone back in the box and return it to the store! He taught me: you don't spend money as soon as you get it just because you have it. You learn to deny yourself the urge to spend so you can truly use your money wisely and not waste it. My dad taught me it was one of the many differences between wealthy thinking and poverty thinking. After that lesson, I no longer wanted the phone.

Remember the five keys to developing kids who POW.

What is your attitude towards saving? Is it something that is a priority to you, or is it something you've never really been good at?

To teach about saving money, it's crucial that you are actively saving money, too. How can you successfully teach what you're not doing yourself? Some of you may say: "I know how to save money, I just don't." My reply is simple: "To know and not to do, is not to know."

The habit of saving money may be challenging for a child—heck, it's hard for most adults. Be patient with your children as they learn to control the urge to spend all their money. We all know this takes practice.

As usual, love them through the mistakes and your frustrations. Shower praise when they meet a savings goal. Reward their hard fought efforts.

As you may know, a savings plan is extremely important. Look at some of the ideas we have below.

Here are a few tips to get kids saving fast:

I.R.S.

IDEAS RECOMMENDATION SOLUTIONS

---

1. **Matching** is probably the fastest way to incentivize kids to save their hard-earned cash. If children know that a certain amount of their money will be matched by putting it away, it will not only motivate them, but it will also help them understand a lot easier certain aspects of the next pillar we plan to discuss.

2. **Open a bank account.** Not only will the kid think it's cool to say they have one, but they'll enjoy going to the bank more than to just get some candy out of the bowl. More importantly, if they can't get to their cash, they're less likely to spend it.

3. **Set goals.** Why is your kid saving money? Make short-term and long-term goals relative to your children's ages. It doesn't have to be complicated. Goals create opportunities for you to motivate your children and keep them focused. Also, goals help children learn to manage their money effectively.

4. **Make it fun!** Saving money should be fun for kids, not full of stress and frustration. Make it fun, and they'll always be interested. Bottom line.

PILLAR #3: TEACHING YOUR KIDS TO INVEST THEIR MONEY.

What's better than saving money? Well, saving even more money and investing some, of course! What is investing? Investing is simply putting something in, to yield a greater return later. A life principle that comes to mind is sowing seed (literally and figuratively). For example, if I sow an apple seed and it produces a tree, do I get one apple? No, I get thousands over time! This basic concept can make it simple for children to understand investing and will give them an edge, because your child will understand from the example that investing takes time and patience. Additionally, there are so many analogies to use like investing time, talents and more when trying to educate a child on what investing is and its value.

Why is investing money so cool? Well, there are many reasons, but one of the coolest is that by investing your money, your money actually starts working for you. Saving money builds security, but investing money can make you wealthy. How cool will it be when your children understand they're making money while going to school because they have investments somewhere? Pretty cool, right?

There are so many different ways to invest money and, as the children you're coaching get older, you can get into all the ways to invest. For now, keep it simple.

Remember five keys to developing kids who POW.

What is your attitude towards investing money? Make sure you have a positive perspective when teaching your children.

Make sure you have something invested when talking to your children. Most people have a 401k or something to reference. If you do not, this will be an awesome project to do with your children. You can find an investment together.

Investing is all about patience and delayed gratification. Be patient teaching your children to have patience with seeing their money again...it may be a while...it may be never depending on the investment.

Have a solid plan for investing money. Be sure to seek a credible financial professional counsel, if needed.

I.R.S.

IDEAS RECOMMENDATION SOLUTIONS

One of the best ways to show children how to invest and how to see their ROI (Return On Investment) faster is to have them start a business. Although it's not the same as investing in stocks or mutual funds, which is considered more passive income, starting a business is more hands-on and (if you're not too familiar yourself or your child may not understand clearly) keeps you from having to figure out and explain the complexities of different types of investing.

For example, on a Friday have your child earn $10 or take $10 from his/her savings. Go on Google and get a nice beverage recipe you want to make and sell. Find a location with some good foot traffic, set up a table, a couple of chairs and sell the beverage for a dollar per cup. By Sunday, your child should have made back his/her investment and much more.

PILLAR #4: TEACHING YOUR KIDS ABOUT CREDIT.

Consumer Credit is an interesting conversation that comes with many views and perspectives. Regardless of the views, it's still something that must be taught to children. I believe the life principle here is one that can fortify one's character or damage it.

Credit starts in the home. What is credit? Credit is simply doing what you've said you would do: Yes, I promise to pay back my loan on time. Yes, mom, I will clean my room when I get home. Credit is simply a measure of character on paper.

When dealing with credit, when you consistently do what you've promised, your score goes up and when you do the opposite, it does down—fast. Teaching kids about credit starts with first teaching them about how to keep their word with those they come in contact with on a daily basis.

When children are enlightened with the value of keeping their word and that character trait is enforced at home, paying a mortgage on time will be easy...barring an uncontrollable situation.

Teaching children to have "good credit," will not only help them develop character, but it will also help with developing sound critical thinking skills. With enough opportunities to learn what "good credit" is and what it is not, children will learn to stop and think before they make an agreement and ask themselves a series of questions like" can I deliver what I'm promising." Teaching the basic concept of credit now will help children avoid a world of turmoil in the future.

Remember the five keys to developing kids who POW.

Persevere Overcome Win!

What is your attitude on credit? How good is your credit? Whether your credit is good or challenged, you have some things you can teach.

Fortunately for some, great credit is not a requirement for teaching this section. I can hear the sighs! LOL! The key is to teach the principles behind having good credit and use them to formulate your training.

This project will test your patience if you're not careful. When doing the exercises I suggested below, do not get frustrated with kids who have continuously bad credit. Help them figure out how to get out of the hole.

Be a nice bill collector if you must be one—especially if you want your child to answer the phone when you call! LOL

As usual, have a plan and work the plan. See the ideas below.

I.R.S.

IDEAS RECOMMENDATION SOLUTIONS

A great way to teach a child about credit is to do it the same way credit bureaus do with the consumer. After teaching your child how financial credit and the moral concept are similar, play a credit score game.

1. Start your child with a "Credit Score" of say 25 with a scale of 5-40 if they're young and maybe 650 with a scale of 550-800 if they're old enough to understand how true credit scores are ranked. It's important to start them off without perfect credit or poor credit so that they understand how their decisions may affect their score

2. Set criteria for things that increase their credit scores and things that reduce it. For example you may say to a younger child: making your bed each day this week will increase your score 10 points and reduce it by 15 for not doing it. Getting in bed by 8:30pm will increase your score by 15 points and reduce it by 15 points every 10 minutes. For an older child you can do the same game and just complicate the criteria according to what you agree upon.

3. The key is to get children to agree to carrying out a task and showing them what happens when they do, and do not, keep their word.

4. There should be an award and denial system set up just as the credit system works. So, if your children obtain a certain score, maybe they have more privileges in a particular area and if their score lowers, maybe they lose some things. The idea is to keep it fun and funny and not something where they lose the importance of learning. Kids with great credit may get to pick their favorite radio station for the week. Kids with poor credit may have to listen to your favorite station. Play the game for a week.

LEARNING TOGETHER:

Teaching our children to become financially literate early on will strengthen their ability to be financially successful later as adults. The four pillars of money give you a place to start investigating and researching more about economics, finance and investing yourself. The beauty of teaching about money is the more you teach it the more you will learn, too. Don't be afraid to learn with your child; it will make the journey more enjoyable for the both of you. Things like playing board games or video games that involve the concepts of the pillars are a great way to learn as a family. Get going and give your child an edge in life!

17

SUCCESSFUL HABITS WITH YOUR KIDS:

Four Habits for Creating the Environment & Exposures you want for your children!

The right environment and the right types of exposures are both relative...only you can decide what is proper for your child. However, both are extremely crucial to a child's success. Photo: some of our campers head to explore the Carnegie Mansion Ruins on the Georgia coast.

It was once said, "We become who we are based on the environment we're in and the things we're exposed to." If you look around, there's a lot of truth to this idea. To be positive, the children of today have access to more information than thirty years ago. However, on the other side, the children of today have more access to more NEGATIVE information than they did 30 years ago, too...and so do you.

The increased amount of information and situations our children are exposed to means there's a greater demand for parents to educate their children. Yes, the already over-worked, pick her up from ballet, drop him off to soccer and have some semblance of dinner ready before bed parent now has to spend more time teaching and explaining what their children are learning at school, with their friends and on social media!

So, what do we do? Hide our kids from the evolving world to protect them from the flood of exposure? Or, should we toss them into the deep end of the pool and wait for their little heads to pop up as they begin to doggy paddle? The answer is YES! There is a way to do both without going overboard. That is what I am going to show you in this section.

There are four habits you must develop in order to manage the kinds of things your children are regularly exposed to and the type of environment you want your children raised in. Each aspect is the responsibility of the VTL to nurture and figure out how to best implement.

18

MORE IMPORTANT THAN MONEY:

#1 The Habit of Quality Time!

Father and son checking the briar on a hunt and learn...Priceless.

This is perhaps the most important of all patterns. **There is no greater investment of your time than the quality time you spend with your own children**. Quality time far outweighs any amount of money you can give. If you're an educator, the time you put into a motivated child today could be the crucial brick that builds the next community or world leader. The quality moments you spend with children can keep them from turning down a dark path in life, or give them the inspiration to create an idea that may change the world.

It reminds me of Rick M. a parent of two adopted children and a middle school teacher from Alabama who decided to follow in the footsteps of his parents who were also teachers and had adopted him and his brother. When they adopted Rick he was in the 5th grade and could barely read or write. What inspired Rick so much was his adopted mother, who was an English teacher. She took the time each night and taught Rick how to read and write until he was a proficient reader. Just think, the choice of one person to invest a little time is now benefiting children of the next generation. That's powerful stuff! What you do today by investing a few more minutes into the lives of your children could have effects for years to come, for children you may never know.

Quality time DOES NOT mean: giving kids money to go spend, while you go work in the office. No, quality time means doing something with your children without outside interruptions or distractions.

Quality time means taking uninterrupted time at the dinner table to discuss their day—without your cell phone being present. It means, board games TOGETHER WITHOUT DISTRACTIONS, video games TOGETHER WITHOUT DISTRACTIONS, taking a walk TOGETHER WITHOUT DISTRACTIONS—anything TOGETHER WITHOUT DISTRACTIONS! Are you catching the main idea here? I've been working with children for many years. I've seen rich parents and broke ones. I've met parents who deserve a medal and ones who should be locked in a cage and forced to fight a pissed-off Iron Mike Tyson. You can normally recognize parents who have a vested interest in their children's future by the quality time they actually spend with their seed(s). What's the point of taking your kids to the park if you stay on the phone the entire time? Realize it or not, it sends the message you don't want which is: I'd rather be doing something else than spending time with you."

Let's put it into perspective:

Over the next week, track how much uninterrupted time you get with your children. Most of you will be fortunate to get three hours each day. Remember, quality time is without all the distractions of the phone and work.

Now, if you get three hours each day, that's 21 hours out of 168 hours in a full week. That means in a full week, you get to spend a wimpy12.5% of the week or less than one full day with your child each week! So, you have to squeeze teaching the values and principles you want your child to have into a very small amount of time. Many of us spend 8-16 hours a day on our jobs and maybe 2-3 hours a day (if we're lucky) with our children. Making minor adjustments in your schedule to be able to give more quality time… will pay off big down the road. Make the best of it!

If one spouse/partner is always working to be the bread winner while the other is trying to build relationships with the children, it makes understanding the children that much harder—your 1950's strategy will have you stretched out on someone's couch trying to figure out where you went wrong. Does this mean less golf? Yes. Will you be a little more tired? Possibly. Will you cherish the memories and will your kid(s) appreciate it? Abso-freakin-lutly!

Today's parents must be hands-on if you're going to rear your children in the direction you want them to go. One of the biggest benefits of quality time is you as a VTL get the chance to learn about your children's strengths and weaknesses so that you know where to lead them and when to redirect them.

19

THE ADVENTURER CALLED: YOU

#2 the Habit of Leading the "Expedition"

Most children love going on adventures. There's no greater way to fire up the mind than to expose all the senses to new and exciting things. Photo: taking a quick break before heading up the mountain.

Exposing children has a lot to do with the senses. What are they seeing, hearing, feeling (emotionally or physically) and so on? What are they watching on social media and what are they engaged in? More importantly, how are they responding as a result of these interactions?

Persevere Overcome Win!

Most of the things children are being exposed to are without your supervision. You REALLY don't know what they're seeing at school, daycare or at practice each day. While this thought is un-nerving for some, there is a way to get in front of some elements your child will face.

Growing up, I used to really enjoy watching Indiana Jones movies. I liked all the wild situations Indy would have to figure out, escape from or navigate through. To add to the suspense, Indiana had a crew of weaker, less knowledgeable people who were eager to assist but often became dependent on him, too.

Does this sound familiar? Think of yourself as a Dr. Jones. It doesn't matter whether you're a teacher, counselor or parent. You have a crew that's on an adventure with you and their lives are in your hands.

I remember a particular scene in the Temple of Doom where Indiana Jones and his crew were eating dinner at the Pankot Palace. The meal had all sorts of exotic dishes like beetles, live snakes and steamed monkey brains (sitting in a decapitated monkey's head, might I add). All the men at the table began to dig in and feast. If you've ever seen the movie, "Short Round" (Indy's young sidekick) eyes were as big as saucers and Willie (Indiana's love interest) just passes out!

What's the point? The take-a-way is Indiana Jones' crew had never been exposed to food of that sort. Fortunately, they were with someone who was familiar and therefore was able to guide them through the situation: eat this, don't eat that, nibble on this et cetera. Now imagine what their experience may have been like if they ran into an unusual dinner on their own without Dr. Jones?

Leading the exposition is taking children and exposing them to situations and things with the safety and security of a mature and knowledgeable adult. Don't let your child find a gun with a friend and risk the unthinkable; take them to a firearm accident prevention class so they know exactly what to do should they find a gun. Instead of your 13-year-old experimenting with heroin after school—unaware of the consequences, watch a documentary on drugs with them and discuss it afterwards.

Some parents and professionals prefer the "don't talk about it and it goes away approach." I'm sorry, for starters this rarely works and secondly, you're not an ostrich! Sticking your head in the sand attempting to ignore the situation, leaves your butt out to be kicked by life's cruel situations!

Get in front of the concerns you may have by exposing your children to them first. That way you have the opportunity to explain how the situation lines up or does not line up with the values you're teaching at home. Now, of course, use common since, that doesn't mean slam your kid's hand on a hot oven to prove it's hot, but I do mean methodically and carefully show them the world they're living in.

Your children will be more prepared to battle what lies ahead because they will be able to use the situations you've taught them as a reference.

In addition to carefully and methodically exposing your children to the "issues" in this world, there's an even greater benefit to exposing them to all the wonders the world has to offer. I am often surprised how many students of mine have never seen the ocean or haven't been in the woods! Many children have yet to see a beautiful sunset, travel outside their city or travel on a plane.

Exposing children to a myriad of activities, sports, hobbies and travel opportunities, expands their imaginations and provides them with options to find interests. I sometimes cringe when I do a teaching session and a large majority of the boys in the room want to be a basketball player, football player or entertainer—rapper to be more specific. There's nothing wrong with the careers, but I often wonder how many of the boys have truly been exposed to more than "what appears easy but is actually very difficult to do"?

Photo: Hiking down from the tundra in the Rocky Mountains trying to beat a storm. We had over 70 super excited teens. It was like trying to herd cats, but so much fun!

On the other hand, I do have many families I work with who do expose their children to all sorts of cool adventures, sports and activities. I have parents, single and two-parent homes, who take their kids, hiking, camping, fishing, horseback riding on vacations, et cetera. YOU CAN SEE THE DIFFERENCE! They hold well-rounded conversations and have a higher level of understanding and are less fearful.

MANAGE WHAT YOUR CHILDREN HEAR

I love music. All kinds of music, and I love Hip-Hop. People listen to the music that best supports their current mood or interest. Why else do we play Prince, Adele, or John Meyer if not to set the mood? Hip Hop legend and rapper Snoop Dogg has some great hits but don't expect your Sunday morning worship choir to sing Gin and Juice as the leading song before the pastor gets up.

Wait, I know this may be hard for some to digest. I'm sorry, sometimes the truth hurts. "I can lie to you, make it sound fly to you," like a verse from rap group Goodie Mob but what will that do? Nothing good. If you don't believe music and media have that much control over thoughts try this game:

For the next three days I want you to listen to three variations of music. Listen to only one genre each day. From the moment you start your morning routine and throughout the day listen to 10 songs. If you want to make it interesting, try music you'd normally not listen to. Now, take notes and journal how you feel by the end of each day and what thoughts you have. You will notice your mood will indeed adjust to what you are hearing. Music uses the power of suggestion.

Censorship is a crucial component and tool that concerned parents must incorporate if they plan to manage what their children see. Yes, they will see things with their friends and no, you can't censor everything. What you can do is control their interest at a young age and attempt to redirect their interest once they're older.

If a movie is rated PG-13 why is your 6-year-old watching it? If, as a parent, you choose to let your child watch certain things or listen to certain music, it may help to have the follow-up conversation that comes with the level of exposure.

20

JUST LIKE U R WHAT U EAT...U WILL B WHAT U C:

#3 The Habit of Creating the Right Environment!

It is the VTL's job to create and monitor the right environment they wish to have their children in. Have you ever seen a child, maybe even your child, do or say something and you respond with, "Where did you learn that?" What a moment, especially when it happens in public! Don't you just love it?!

Children will become what they're exposed to most in their environment. Environment and exposure go hand-in-hand. What is an Environment? Children's environment is the area where they're receiving the greatest influence.

Children have three basic environments where they receive the most influence: home, school, extra-curricular activities (sports, clubs and other social activities). The environments intersect.

The three areas either run in harmony or in chaos. A disruption in one area will ultimately lead to the disruption in another area. Likewise, enough harmony in one area will spill over to another area. Contrary to the belief of some, children are not born with bad behavior. Behavior, good or bad is developed. Many times when a child is expressing unpleasant behavior it's because one of the three areas I mentioned above is out of balance.

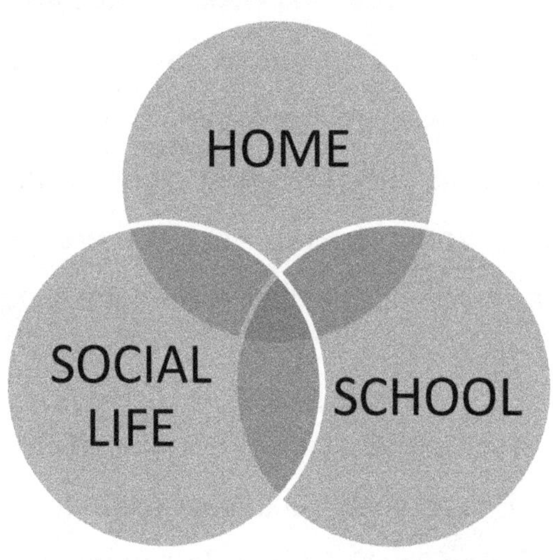

For example, let's say a VTL and his/her child has a really bad argument before she heads off to school. Once in class she realizes the assignment that was due is sitting on the counter at home. Immediately, she thinks if not for the confusion at home, she'd have remembered to bring the assignment—now the teacher will certainly give her an F.

The three areas are where children truly have their best and worst experiences and where their precious lives are formed. In fact, environments play one of the most crucial roles in shaping their dreams or destroying them.

The wrong environment can be like crabs in a barrel where no one gets out because everyone is holding each other down. Or, the right environment can be like a flock of birds…who understand that by working together, everyone can get to their desired destinations. "An environment can help your children or get them in a lot of trouble."

The reason Environment is such a crucial part of developing children who <u>POW</u> is it transcends socio-economic boundaries. The impact of environment is not dependent on color or status. We can have children in a bad community environment—yet have a healthy home environment and they'll do well until they move out. However, the kid who has a great surrounding environment, yet a terrible home environment is in worse danger. Both can make it, but one may have more emotional baggage that will affect future relationships.

For example, children who are abused or witness abuse are more likely to be abusive in the future. Environment and exposure go hand in hand.

As a Village Team Leader, you have a great role in managing your children's environment. Remember the Confidence Castle™? You are the guardian who controls the barriers, and you're the Lookout. So, how do we manage our environment? How do we make sure our children are being exposed to the right things in our community, at practice, at school or in the neighborhood? Drum roll, please! **Parent Involvement!** Did I shock you?

As a kid, I and many of my friends were bussed out to suburban schools as part of an initiative to equalize learning. You can imagine that we were not received with welcoming arms by some of the school staff or the children there.

I remember my mom coming up to my school, smelling like cleaning supplies, driving her maroon "A-Team" van. Mom made it her business to meet with my teachers at a parent conference, attend events when she could and lobby on my behalf.

It didn't matter if it was a game, school or any other event if my parents could make it they would, and when they could not, someone: my sister, cousin, or extended family would be there. Now, there were times that no one could attend a game or activity. It wasn't a big deal because I knew their habits and their hearts.

Parent involvement allows you, the VTL, to monitor your children's activities and to establish a rapport in your children's environment.

A big difference between me and some of the kids I grew up with was I had family involvement. I had people involved in my life and involved with what happened in my life. The major difference in kids succeeding or failing in the 21st century has a lot to do with parent or family involvement.

If a child is being neglected because everyone is too busy—you can bet that boy or girl is going to find some pretty creative ways to get you to pay attention, and you won't like it!

Additionally, the people caring for your child will conduct themselves differently when they know there's an involved parent or family member checking in on a regular basis.

Parent involvement doesn't always mean just showing up. It also means taking the opportunity to actively participate when possible. If there's a bake sale, bring some cookies. If the team needs an assistant coach—volunteer.

Your presence really makes a difference in securing the atmosphere and providing a sense of checks and balances. More importantly, it will mean the world to your children.

Don't you carry yourself a little differently or go the extra mile when you wish to impress someone? Kids do the same thing. They want to make you proud. Some of the best musicians, athletes and intellectuals have a strong core support system.

Want a star? Be actively involved in his/her activities. It doesn't require money, but it does require a little more time.

Another essential aspect of creating the right environment for your child is to **BE SELECTIVE.** Don't just settle for what's in your area if it's not up to par. For example, we have families from all over metro Atlanta who travel to attend Camp Warrior King. Sure, there are plenty of camps closer to their homes, but our families love the service we provide; they know the children are safe and kids have an awesome time.

If you want your children to think "outside the box," you must engage them in activities that stretch their imagination and competitive edge. Photos: our students working their Foil techniques.

Selecting a camp, daycare, school, neighborhood or instructor should be done using the utmost discretion.

Finally, --**INSPECT, INSPECT, INSPECT**. Look around, ask specific questions and get references, if necessary. By asking questions and being thorough you are increasing the likelihood of your child's safety. People who work with your children should not take offense at your diligence. If they do--red flag. I once heard someone say, "People of integrity expect to be believed, and when they're not, they let time prove them right."

Remember that children will conform to the environment they're in. It is almost impossible for a child to Persevere Overcome and Win in an environment where they are constantly subjected to inescapable emotional destruction. Being at the edge requires focus that must be sustained with strong support.

Set the tone and parameters for the Environment your children are in.

As a VTL, you must establish the standard for each environment your children are in—while they are young. Your standard is what gives them standards when they get older.

In the home, if you don't establish the kind of atmosphere that's acceptable and unacceptable early on, you can bet the environment will be out of control and open for influence by anyone who comes through the doors.

For example, growing up talking back to my father was like going to a bar alone in Tuscaloosa Alabama, wearing Auburn gear and talking trash after beating the Tide in the Iron Bowl! Why would you do something so stupid? Yet, I never felt that either of my parents did not love me dearly.

A loving environment in the classroom starts on the first day. A loving camp, team or group, all has to be created by the person leading the group. The standards must not be compromised for any reason. Having standards doesn't mean you're a tyrant, it just means you have standards.

If you allow your children to continue hanging with negative influences after they tell you of the extremely negative things their friends do, you're sending the message that it's not only OK to have those kinds of friends, it's OK to be like them, too.

The beauty is that you can always make a decision right now and set new standards. Change is never too late

What things do you want to redirect or regain control over in the environments your children are in? Write them really fast:

____

____

____

On a separate sheet of paper, write how you will implement them. What has stopped you from doing them before? How do you avoid the pitfall or setback(s) again? Who can help hold you accountable to see the changes through? Make the changes and keep moving.

Teaching your children to love being one of a kind!

Many children today are afraid to stand out. It seems safer to blend in, but there's a great cost to blending in. Take a second and reflect on a moment when you did the opposite of the crowd. Maybe it was going to college or making a decision to move away or play one sport over the other. What were the positives and challenges? What did you learn? How did it make your life better?

____

____

____

____

Now, share this experience with the kids the next time they are making a decision to go against the grain.

As a Village Team Leader you must teach your children there is a price for conforming and going with the trend. Greatness must stand out in order to be recognized as such. I can't tell you how many times my friends and I were called "Nerds," or 'Geeks," because we didn't conform to what "All the other kids were doing." Now, being a nerd, or at least looking like one, is the "In thing." How many kids have killed themselves because they were bullied for being different? The reality is: WE ARE ALL DIFFERENT! We were made different by design, and no two people are exactly the same.

21

HELP THEM OUT OF THE BOX CALLED "COMFORTABLE":

#4 The Habit of Allowing Your Child to Explore

Giving children the opportunity to explore builds trust, communication skills and responsibility. Photo: taking a break from a wildly funny scavenger hunt on a development trip.

As much as it pains us as VTLs we must allow the children we nurture to learn from some experiences on their own. Unfortunately, we don't always get to choose which experiences they're going to be.

Fortunately, the previous three habits, if implemented correctly, will assist you in feeling better about what decisions your children will make on their own and manage the severity of the experience.

When learning to ride a horse, instructors teach that when you fall it's important that you get back up on the horse immediately. If not, the horse may feel as if it's in control and can intimidate you.

The same is true for life situations with the children under our care. In their environment, children will have their own set of challenges and obstacles to overcome. When they come in from the world busted up, bandage the wounds, give them some love, a better strategy and encourage them to get back on the horse!

As a kid I can remember running in our apartment when the sons (who were like older brothers to me) of a close family friend would wrestle a little too roughly. I would tell on them to my mom that they were beating me up when they started to play too roughly! My mother would say, "Tell them I said to stop beating you up." And she'd send me back outside. Being naïve, I did as I was told: "My mommy said stop beating me up!" LOL, you can imagine the results: Bang! Slam! Boom!

I learned early to figure out how to maneuver in the environment I was in. I learned that my mom was not going to be around for every situation I faced, and, therefore, I had to start thinking.

I stopped telling the boys what my mom said (since I think she was setting me up anyway) and started to speak up for myself. When that didn't work—which in my case it only excited them, I learned to fight back.

By allowing your children to explore life in a controlled environment, they learn how to think for themselves, and they learn at an early age to practice what you've taught them. The benefit is they have you to bounce ideas off of, and it allows you to see which strategies work and which need to be restructured.

The children who never get opportunities to explore simply because their VTL wants to shelter them, will be preyed upon. Self-exploration creates enlightenment and self-discovery.

I.R.S.

IDEAS RECOMMENDATION SOLUTIONS

Here are some recommendations and solutions to help you direct or redirect your children in their environment.

1. Manage Your Children's Dealings

Growing up with our friends, our families constantly monitored our dealings and communicated with each other often. Our parents talked to, physically met, and stayed in communication with all of our friends' parents. We also had older cousins and brothers who looked after all of the friends in our group to make sure everyone was safe and out of trouble.

Remember, you are the VTL, don't be afraid to use your authority. Remember, earlier we discussed being your child's friend? Well, kids tell their friends things, and they do not share information with those who are not their friends. So, it's hard to manage if you don't know what's going on. Be a friend and become a better manager.

2. *Help your children mind their business by setting goals and chasing them.*

My friends and I thrived in various environments because we had goals. We saw what was happening to the guys hustling illegally—they weren't coming out too well in the long run. Our goals kept us occupied. We wanted to be in the recording studio, on the football field or in a debate lab somewhere.

We weren't hanging with the kids stealing cars. Of course, we knew them and some were cool people honestly, but we weren't getting in anyone's car with a 13-year-old at the wheel. We were not running to a fight to watch it. That's how you got shot!

To save children living in a challenging environment, they must have goals that keep them too busy for trouble along with an adult to keep them accountable. Yes, it's possible.

3. *Direct your children towards pursuing diverse interests and thinking differently.*

There's a saying, "When you see everyone else doing the same thing…do the opposite!" So many kids are interested in the same things: basketball, football, rapping. Nothing wrong with these activities—we did that, too (although I SUCKED and still SUCK at basketball.)

However we also learned to play instruments, do martial arts, camp, debate and did just about everything else we could find to occupy our time. What we learned was none of the kids getting in trouble were there!

When I started debating in high school, unfortunately it was rare to see many inner-city children at big, national tournaments like the Barkley Forum, Wake Forest or Kentucky tournaments. There were even fewer of these children at the forensic summer camps.

Debate, like chess, forces you to think differently and in a more dynamic fashion. When your children are thinking from a broader perspective with greater exposure they will also be able to navigate through troublesome situations that may normally stump another untrained mind.

To save children living in a challenging environment they must find interests that put them on a different path…a path less traveled. Consider it their personal HOV lane.

4. *Teach Your Children Awareness.*

You can be in a situation and not be of it. As I said earlier, my friends and I were never gang-bangers, or drug dealers, but we knew how to recognize them, and we knew where they hung out. Therefore, we also knew where NOT to be…EVER.

If we had a friend who started stealing, he/she could no longer hang with us. Our parents would not allow it. This is what will save your child: a VTL who is willing to learn strategies to change the course of a child's life when needed.

To save children living in a challenging environment they must be taught to be aware of their surroundings and how to act accordingly.

These four basic ideas and strategies will keep your children headed in the direction you want. Help the children you're working with implement them immediately. Make sure to hold the children accountable.

SET NO LIMITS!

When children have a vision and strong support at home, they become an unstoppable force. Photo: Exceptional Kid Campaign winners honored at our Fall Family Convention. These kids are AMAZINGLY TALENTED!

Your children are blessed to have you in their life. You and the one(s) you serve are designed to be together for a reason. Regardless of what happens, by you putting your best foot forward to help develop and help influence a child, you are making a lasting impression on his/her life. The decisions these children make as adults and the people they will come to have valuable relationships with will be in part because of your influence, leadership and direction.

Persevere Overcome Win!

Don't be afraid to fail, because you won't. Although you may experience failures along the way that does not mean you have failed with the children under your care. It simply means, you've experienced failures, hopefully you will learn from and improve upon them

You've learned the keys to developing a child. Tuck them deeply into your heart so that they arise involuntarily when called upon. When all else fails, remember to love unconditionally. You have been prepared and equipped to make a difference.

Set no limits to the depth or breath of what you can accomplish with the material in this book. Set no limits to what you can do to touch lives around this globe with your personal story and experience.

There are certain children around the world waiting to be inspired and motivated by your gifts, and no one can make them move quite like you.

God bless you and thank you for reading this book. I look forward to meeting you and hearing about how this book has helped you develop and nourish lives wherever you are in the world.

Together, we will develop kids who POW!

Be sure to maximize the advantages of buying this book!

*Take your students, staff and school to the next level. Schedule a presentation for your next professional development workshop.

*Get FREE training videos and access more resources on our website.

*Let us know which concepts helped you, your team and/or your children most. We want to hear from you.

*Do you have a friend, co-worker or know of a school/program the information in this book can provide value to? Share the love and please let them know about this book and the valuable information.

Visit Kidsthatpow.com

Call (678)-408-2053

PO BOX 87401, COLLEGE PARK, GA 30337

BIBLIOGRAPHY

Alexander, Scott. *Rhinoceros Success.* Laguna Hill, CA: 1980.

Bronson, Po and Ashley Merryman. *Nurture Shock.* New York:Twelve, 2009.

Brown, Les. *Live Your Dreams.* New York: Morrow Books, 1

Canfield, Jack, Mark Victor Hansen and Les Hewitt. *The Power of Focus.* Deerfield Beach, FL: 0 Health Communications Inc., 2000.

Chapman, Gary D. *The 5 Love Languages of Children.* Chicago, IL.: 2012.

Carnegie, Dale. *How to Win Friends & Influence People.* New York: Simon & Schuster 1981

Clason, George S. The Richest Man in Babylon. New York: Signet, 1988

Cline, Foster and Jim Fay. *Parenting with Love and Logic.* Colorado Springs, CO: Pinon Press, 2006.

Cosby, Bill. *Fatherhood.* New York: Berkley Book, 1986.

Covey, Stephen R. *The 7 Habits of Highly Effective People.* New York, NY: Fireside, 1990.

Delpit, Lisa. *Other People's Children.* New York, NY: The New Press, 1995.

Dobson, James. *Temper Your Child's Tantrum.* Carol Streams, IL: Tyndale House Publishers, 1986.

Dollar, Creflo and Taffi Dollar. *The Successful Family.* College Park, GA: Creflo Dollar Ministries, 2002

Dungy, Tony. *Quiet Strength*. Carol Stream, IL: Tyndale House Publishers, 2007.

Dyson, Michael Eric. *Know What I Mean?* New York, NY: Basic Civitas Books, 2007.

Faber, Adele and Elaine Mazlish. *How to Talk So Kids Will Listen & Listen So Kids Will Talk*. New York, NY: HarperCollins, 1999.

Galinsky, Ellen. *Mind in the Making*. New York, NY: HarperCollins, 2010.

Getty, J. Paul. *How to be Rich*. New York, NY: The Berkley Publishing Group, 1966.

Graham, Billy. *Just As I Am*. New York, NY: HarperCollins, 1997.

Hill, Napoleon. *Think and Grow Rich*. Hollywood, CA: The Napoleon Hill Foundation,1966.

Hilliard, Asa. *SBA: The Reawakening of the African Mind*. Gainesville, FL: Makare Publishing, 1998.

Jay-Z. *Decoded*. New York, NY: Spiegel & Grau: 2010.

Peale, Norman, V. *The Power of Positive Thinking*. New York, NY: Fawcett Crest, 1982.

Price, Hugh B. *Achievement Matters*. New York, NY: Kensington Publishing Corp,, 2002.

Robbins, Anthony *Unlimited Power*. London: Simon & Schuster, 1998.

Shor, Ira. *Freire for the Classroom*. Portsmouth, NH: Boynton/Cook, 1987.

Senior, Jennifer. *All Joy and No Fun*. New York, NY: HarperCollins, 2014.

Siegel, Daniel J., M.D. and Tina Payne Bryson, M.D. *The Whole Brain Child.* New York: Bantam Books, 2012.

Simmons, Russell. *Do You!* New York, NY: Gotham Books, 2007.

Simmons, Russell. *Super Rich.* New York, NY: Gothan Books, 2011.

Schwartz, David Joseph. *The Magic of Thinking Big.* New York: Simon & Schuster, 1987.

Wigglesworth, Smith. *The Power of Unlimited Faith.* New Kensington, PA: Whitaker House 1998

Yager, Dexter, *Don't Let Anybody Steal Your Dream.* Springfield, MO: Restoration, 1978.

Zink, J. *Champions in the* Making; U.S.A. Dr. J. Zink, 1983.

Zondervan. *The Amplified Bible and the King James Bible.* Grand Rapids, MI, 1995

About the Author

Performance enhancer, author and businessman Shaun "SF" Banks is revolutionizing the personal development industry with high-powered, creative and results-driven books, videos, workshops and presentations.

Shaun is quickly becoming the go-to guy for organizations like yours who want to be certain their groups are not only motivated to act after a great teaching session but, more importantly, walk away with useful and applicable knowledge. His development strategies can be put to use immediately for improved quantifiable and qualitative results.

Shaun has literally assisted thousands of children and their families, helping them develop realistic, tailor-made and easy to implement strategies in areas such as competitive performance, personal growth, optimal health, improved self-esteem, heightened focus, discipline, quick action-taking and goal setting.

www.ingramcontent.com/pod-product-compliance
Lightning Source LLC
LaVergne TN
LVHW011227080426
835509LV00005B/371